FOR UNTO US

To Anna & Steve –
God bless you always
and in all ways.

[signature] 2014

For Unto Us

Lessons from the Life of Jesus

Timothy L. Owings

SMYTH&HELWYS
PUBLISHING INCORPORATED • MACON, GEORGIA

Smyth & Helwys Publishing, Inc.
6316 Peake Road
Macon, Georgia 31210-3960
1-800-747-3016
©2004 by Smyth & Helwys Publishing
All rights reserved.
Printed in the United States of America.

The paper used in this publication meets the minimum requirements of
American National Standard for Information Sciences—
Permanence of Paper for Printed Library Materials.
ANSI Z39.48–1984. (alk. paper)

Library of Congress Cataloging-in-Publication Data

Owings, Timothy.
For unto us : lessons from the life of Jesus
by Timothy L. Owings.
p. cm.
ISBN 1-57312-444-3 (pbk. : alk. paper)

1. Jesus Christ—Biography—Sermons.
2. Church year sermons.
3. Baptists—Sermons.
4. Sermons, American.
I. Title.
BT306.33.O94 2004
252'.6—dc22

2004024128

Across the span of two millennia, the life of Jesus continues to speak of uncommon love and transforming acceptance. No other figure in human history has attracted so much interest, summoned so much devotion, or created so much controversy. The mere mention of the name "Jesus" stirs the pot of public and private opinion to the point of a fevered boil. Scholars and preachers, theologians and film makers, the faithful and the fretful all find common cause invoking his name to endorse an idea, season a movement, or pacify a conscience. Jesus is the one person in history around whom the human family still finds hope, inspiration, courage, and joy. His life, death, and resurrection stand as the singular moment around which our calendar revolves and, for Christians, our lives turn.

For many in the Christian family, the Christian year begins with the season of Advent and continues through the seasons of Christmastide, Epiphany, Lent, Easter, and Pentecost. Five of the six seasons focus on our Lord's life: his coming in history and in glory, his life, death, and resurrection. In these five seasons, from late fall to spring, Christian believers hear the invitation once again to follow our Lord. He is the one who goes before us in life, in death, and in life after death.

This collection of twenty-five lessons I have called *For Unto Us* is an attempt, albeit halting and incomplete, to journey through these five seasons using the Scriptures as our trusted guide. Every one of these reflections was preached as part of a sermon series at the First Baptist Church of Augusta, Georgia, where I had the privilege and rare joy of being pastor for thirteen years. There, the gracious and engaged people of God encouraged me week after week to find the new in the good news. There, without any agenda or compulsion, the people gathered to listen prayerfully as I led them in worship through the preaching of the gospel. There, young and old, black, white, and Asian, rich and poor, the seasoned of faith and those just starting the journey called me to be my best self. There, much grace was given and much love exchanged as pastor and people listened with expectancy to what God was saying through Scripture, prayer, music, and that still, small voice of the Spirit.

The twenty-five reflections that follow are grouped into four categories. The first section, "Beginnings," takes us from those first announcements of the coming Messiah in Advent through the birth of our Lord in Bethlehem. These are the moments from the text when we first hear heaven's rumblings about the coming of one who topples kings from their thrones while gently finding his way into the sacred spaces of the human heart. In this section, I have taken great liberty to focus on Mary, the mother of our Lord. Long neglected in Protestant preaching, Mary is still the first witness to Jesus. Her naïve courage, her tender openness, and her gracious "Yes" speak across the ages to those of us who let fear cripple us rather than call us. The characters who precede the birth of the Messiah like the prophets, Mary, Joseph, John the Baptist, Elizabeth, and Zechariah show us the best way toward the stable in Bethlehem.

A collection of five reflections titled "Teach Us to Pray" comprise section two of this volume. The Model Prayer has long held a revered and trusted place in our hearts and liturgy. My Christian experience has been nourished by simply praying this prayer and finding in it a trusted guide in my journey with the Holy One. In this section, I have included five pastoral prayers from my ministry at Augusta's First Baptist Church.

The third section contains reflections on our Lord's teaching ministry. Often, Jesus would say, "those who have ears, listen." So I have called this section "Ears that Hear." Too often, we read the biblical text but either do not hear or refuse to hear what God is saying to us. In my judgment, our problem with Jesus' teaching is not that we fail to understand him. To the contrary, having understood well what he has taught, we refuse to follow his teaching or live by his word. I have included sermons here from texts in the Sermon on the Mount, Jesus' public ministry of healing and mighty works, and the parables.

The final section is "Journey Into Life," inviting us to walk those last days of our Lord's ministry to Jerusalem, the cross, and the empty tomb. God's good news in Jesus Christ is a journey into life from all that is death and death dealing. Whether we are crippled by prejudice, wounded by failure, hurt by another's insensitivity, or angered by injustice, Jesus calls us from all that destroys and kills us to all that is in him that gives us life. His death, burial, and resurrection reveal to us the full measure of God's unrequited, amazing love. No tomb can contain it, no creed control it, no belligerence stop it. "O the deep, deep love of Jesus, vast, unmeasured, boundless free! Rolling as a mighty ocean in its fullness over me; underneath me, all around me is the current of Thy love; leading onward, leading homeward, to my glorious rest above."

The editing of this book for final publication has come at a pivotal time in my life. In June 2003, I resigned the pastorate of First Baptist Church of Augusta, believing my ministry there had come to an end. It was a painful departure for me, my family, and so many within that wonderful, loving congregation and the Augusta community. Four months later, my father, having just reached his eighty-fourth birthday, passed from this life into life eternal. Within six weeks of my dad's death, I began a new work with Resource Services, Inc. (RSI) in Dallas, Texas, consulting with churches, helping them raise needed capital to expand their ministries and further their mission. The months leading up to completing *For Unto Us* have been filled with loss, change, renewal, and much hope.

In many ways, the completing of this project has reengaged my life and heart with the life and teaching of our Lord. Though I have been preaching for more than thirty years, I have come to these texts with new eyes and renewed conviction. Loss, death, and change have a powerful way in our lives either to ennoble us or crush us. Though I have often considered letting the pain crush me, I can still hear my father remind me that the best is always yet to be. He believed that because he had a relationship with Christ. And because he did, I have found great strength in learning from his struggle and victory.

Finally, I must thank many people for encouraging me to complete *For Unto Us*. Hundreds of members of Augusta's First Baptist Church and many more in Augusta and surrounding communities have blessed my life with generous affirmation. Their prayers, support, and interest in my preaching and writing ministry have gently and faithfully nudged me to bring this book to completion. Thank you. The good pastor of the First Baptist Church, Twin City, Georgia, Rev. M. Franklin Sasser, graciously invited me to preach a Lenten revival in March 2004, giving me precious time at his pond house to complete this manuscript. Thank you, Franklin, for warm and generous time and solitude.

The initial transcribing of these reflections was the work of my exceptional secretary of twelve years, Mrs. Dede Maddox. Dede's support, prayers, and constant encouragement have often turned on the sunshine in what were dark days. Most of all, I thank my wife and family for the gifts of love, support, and grace. Kathie and I have shared so much of life, both the joyous and the sad, the wonder and the terror, that I could not imagine doing life without her. Hers is a love that, thank God, has never let me go. And yes, in the love of an amazingly courageous family, at first our three children and now enlarging to include more with more love, I have found great strength and nourishing hope.

To those who wonder if Jesus' life, teaching, passion, and resurrection still have meaning today, I can only point to lives changed week by week in congregations and communities around the world who follow and worship God as revealed in Jesus Christ. The witness of the church universal is still that simple confession of faith: Christ has died, Christ is risen, Christ will come again. Even so, come, Lord Jesus. Come to us who still long for the new in the good news, and lead us from everything that is dark and dying into that light is life eternal.

Lent 2004

Beginnings

Shaking Heaven and Earth

On that day the LORD will be one and his name one.
—Zechariah 14:9

When I come to the first Sunday in Advent, this Sunday at the beginning of the church's liturgical year, my soul reminds me that something new is in the air. Thanksgiving is now history and the Sundays of "ordinary time" are behind us as the church begins her preparation for Christmas. Long ago, Christian believers started a journey the four Sundays before Christmas. To this journey, they gave the name Advent, meaning "coming."

Advent sways in two directions. On one side, it pulls us with wide-eyed wonder toward the feast of Christmas, the birth of our Lord. Christmas invites, woos, beckons us with nearly irresistible power. On the other side, feeling strange to us, at least at first, is Jesus' second coming in glory. There we are, called to make the Advent journey, pulled in both directions. And yet, we who relish the wonder of Christmas are not completely sure how to prepare for our Lord's return. Pulled in both directions, the season bids us to do the less-than-entrancing work of preparing for our Lord's return while lulling us into wonder beneath a caroled sky and before a decorated tree. When we come to church the first Sunday in Advent, we hear strange Scriptures read that seem to have little if anything to do with Christmas.

In a word, Advent says "Wait." One of the great challenges for Christians during Advent is to hold back the celebration of the birth of Jesus, to wait, to anticipate in order to hear fully the promise of Jesus' second coming. In a day when the Christmas merchandise is out weeks before Halloween, when the year past cries out for some tinseled wonder, it is difficult to wait.

The prophet Zechariah and the evangelist Luke both wrote stark descriptions of last things. I don't know how deeply these words sink into your mind, but Zechariah 14:4-9 is radically apocalyptic, boiling with end-time promises. Like Advent, these lines speak of fear and wonder. The prophet spoke of the Mount of Olives to the east of Jerusalem being hewn in two by a rupturing earthquake. One side will move to the south and the other side to the north. And yet, beyond this shaking of heaven and earth is an idyllic time when "the LORD will become king over all the earth," that moment when, at the end, Messiah comes.

The text also talks about waters flowing out from Jerusalem; waters to the eastern sea and waters to the western sea, a sign of productivity and newness. Yet this word of newness can be drowned out by earthquake shaking with mountains divided, the heavens trembling, the earth split. That's what we hear. In doing so, we may miss the good news within and around these words.

A similar scenario meets us at Luke 21:25-31 as Jesus speaks to his disciples. He talks about that moment when time and history will come to an end. Jesus said there will be signs in the sun, the moon, and the stars. There will be distress among nations. People will faint with fear. Dread will be the order of the day. Sounds almost like the morning newspaper, doesn't it? Jesus saw that moment when history will end and the kingdom of God will come in all of its fullness.

We live in such an odd day, don't we? We live in what could be described as an awesome opportunity in history made possible by technology. I'm told the computer chip is doubling its speed every twenty-four months. I don't know whether you can do the numbers on that, but that means every twenty-four months, the speed with which we process data doubles. For example, in the year 2000, I purchased a computer that runs at the speed of 700 megahertz. The standard today—in 2004—is at 2.4 gigahertz and growing, more than three times the speed I bought four years ago.

We live in a day of awesome opportunity. Anyone with a computer, a modem, and an Internet service provider can communicate with anyone else in the world instantly. When you plug into the Internet, you have at your fingertips a global communication resource. My good friend, Dr. Harry Lucenay presently serves as pastor of a church in Hong Kong. Harry and I often e-mail each other halfway around the world. He writes me from tomorrow; I answer him from yesterday. What an incredible, fascinating day in which to live. This is a day of unprecedented global economic and political opportunity. We stagger to think what the human mind can conceive and create in order to bring people together around the world. Ours is an awesome time in the wide scope of human history.

Ours is also an ominous time. The problem of human hunger has not disappeared. AIDS is devastating the continent of Africa. War and its aftermath seem like tenured residents in the middle east. Though we don't know physical hunger so much in this country as in other nations, we share a hunger *for meaning* with other developed nations. Mother Teresa, now of blessed memory, was right about so many things. She said the great hunger in the West is for meaning—for relationships, for love, for value in human life. Ours is also a brutal time when violence and fear and, in some corners of the world, savagery are making the human species look more like animals than human beings. We have so much in a world where so many have so little.

What are these Scriptures across the span of more than two millennia saying to us? Why would we read texts that talk about earth and heaven shaking? This shaking of heaven and earth rumbles the foundations beneath us and lowers the ceilings above us. These verses remind us that often, our lives are spiritually, emotionally, and relationally crushed. Both Jesus and Zechariah knew that. When there is a shaking of heaven and earth, every molecule within us wants to retreat, to withdraw, to give up. Everything within us wants to move into the fetal position. Is there a good word from God for such a day as this?

Jesus gave his disciples a good word, good news for them and for us. "Fear," said our Lord, "is not to be the posture of the believer. When you see heaven and earth shake, when you sense the world coming to an end, when what you think is important dissolves around you, think not that it is a time to retreat into yourself. Rather, imagine the moment as a time to lift up your heads." Note our Lord's word choices. "When you see these things happening [not *if you see them*]." The Bible does not raise the question of whether or not heaven and earth are going to shake. Write it down. Heaven and earth will shake sometime for you. For some of us, it shakes more often than we would like it to shake. The question is not "If" but "When."

What is Jesus saying? "When you see these things happen," don't buy into the prevailing wisdom of the day. Don't purchase the pervasive fear being sold. Lift up your heads; your redemption is coming near. What a shocking thing to say. What a "Pollyanna" pronouncement. What a seemingly ridiculous thing to believe. You mean when everything about me is falling apart, I'm supposed to stand up, lift up, and look up? That's what Jesus said. That's ridiculous; it doesn't make sense. Everything within us says such a posture is nonsense. Why? Because when our world falls apart, the natural inclination is to withdraw, to check out, to give up.

What do we of faith do when we sense heaven and earth shaking? What do we do? The Scriptures tell us that we who believe can lift up our heads because God is coming near.

Seems like yesterday that the newspapers were full of "Y2K" stories spinning out doomsday scenarios. As in generations past, many Christians rallied to the advent of the third millennium as the time when Christ will return. But alas, no sooner has the ink dried on newsprint than yet another prediction lies crumbled on the floor. Mind you, I anticipate the second coming of our Lord as that moment when history will come to a consummating end followed by the fullness of the kingdom of God. I am less convinced that any of our end-time scenarios are accurate, much less helpful. I am confident that God will bring about history's end in God's way, in God's time, in God's love. With the Church historic I confess, "Christ has died, Christ is risen, Christ will come again." I take no issue with anyone's end-time theological perspective. But I do suggest that there is within all of us a longing, a hope, and a need to see what is present in this world transformed, if not by the coming of Jesus, by something. And for Christians, our hope is that God is coming, God is moving our way. Whether you understand that to be in the next three years or in the next three millennia is really a moot point. For people of faith, God is always drawing near. God is always coming with transforming love.

Jesus' first sermon—that powerful two-line sermon he preached as recorded in Mark 1:15—set the tone for his entire ministry. Our Lord was walking along the seashore one day when he said, "The time is fulfilled, and the kingdom of God has come near; repent, and believe in the good news." The kingdom of God had come touchably near in Jesus' life, death, and resurrection; this is bedrock Christian teaching. Beyond that, however, we must tread softly and listen carefully. Jesus clearly stated that he didn't know when time would be no more. He said (if I could paraphrase), "I don't have a clue when the kingdom of God will come in all of its fullness. Not even the angels know that. Only God" (Mark 13:32).

But I do know this. Regardless of how your world looks today or how it feels or whatever the circumstances are in your life, whether they be wonderful or terrible, God is drawing near to you. God is present to you. Lift up your head. Your redemption is drawing near.

The text says something else. "Lift up your heads" because redemption, not destruction, is the last word. The last word about life in God's dictionary is always redemption, not destruction. All my life, from the time I was very small, I've heard sermons preached about the second coming of Jesus Christ. I've benefited from many of those sermons. I've either been inspired or informed. My horizons have been expanded, and my hope has been enlarged by sermons I've heard or read that explore the coming of Jesus. The hope contained in the promise of our Lord's return is every Christian's birthright. But there is a great danger today lurking among the Christian family. Those of us who anticipate with hope the second coming of Jesus and his coming in Bethlehem would be wise to listen. Apocalyptic scenarios—armies amassed on the plains of Israel, political scenarios played out in the Middle East, the Far East, and Washington—based upon a verse of Scripture here, a phrase there, and an idea somewhere else are dangerously incomplete. Why? Because the fantastic scenarios that many people imagine concerning the coming of Jesus major more on destruction than on redemption. We who are Christian need always remember that the coming One comes to redeem the world from its death and its destruction, its sin and its hell. The last word is not destruction. The last word is redemption.

I've known, as have you through the years, people who are living with the terrifying fear that the last word over their life will be destruction, when in fact, according to Jesus, the last word is redemption. People who have been told they have cancer know this well. As that sinister organism works in the human body to bring about physical destruction, there is that word, that fear, that horror as earth and heaven shake that nothing can be done about it. My friend, if you have had that diagnosis or if someone you love has been given that diagnosis, which in so many terrifying words is in our hearing a death sentence, lift up your heads. The last word in Christ is not the word destruction. The last word is redemption.

Many know the destruction of divorce, the terror brought about in a family when brokenness is everywhere. I've had more than a few friends in the ministry go through the painful experience of a broken home. No doubt you have had friends at work, neighbors, and family members who are either near or in the middle of a divorce. It seems that divorce has affected so many lives. The people with whom I've spoken and the hurt I've heard over the years coming out of the brokenness of divorce is this feeling, this reality of the destruction of that which once was precious and beautiful and fulfilling.

As your heaven and earth shake, there is good news. If you or someone you love is going through or has gone through that destructive shaking of heaven and earth called divorce, lift up your heads. You may be in the throes of a divorce's destructive wrath, but the last word is redemption and grace, forgiveness and hope. Lift up your heads. Redemption is the last word.

There is one last, good word here, a word so important to hear. We are wise to lift up our heads, because there is healing in hope. How many times have you found yourself in a moment when you were absolutely sure that the earth was shaking and the heavens were filled with terror? How many times have you thought to yourself that life was literally falling apart all around you and your natural inclination was to retreat into the pain, live surrounded by the hurt, nurse the brokenness, play to the destruction? Hear Jesus. There is great healing in hope. When heaven and earth shake, when everything within you wants to retreat, withdraw, move into the spiritual fetal position of life, Jesus says, "There is healing in hope. Lift up your heads, redemption is near."

You say, "How does that work?" Let me give you a graphic illustration. Victor Frankl was a survivor of Auschwitz. He died not long ago and, if memory serves me, he died the same day Princess Diana was killed in a traffic accident. He was the creator of the school of psychotherapy called "Logo Therapy." Victor Frankl survived Auschwitz. He wrote a little book called *Man's Search for Meaning* that has been reprinted dozens and dozens of times. The whole thesis of the book is simply this: no matter what circumstances you find yourself in, no matter how difficult life may be, no matter the "What" of your life, whatever it is through which you must live, you can survive and triumph over that experience if you have a "Why" to live.

Frankl noticed that the people who survived the death camp were people who had something undone yet to be finished after the war. There was a half completed book manuscript or a project they were working on professionally that needed their attention after the war. There were things they needed to do beyond the moment, relationships that called them beyond the horror, a "Why," a hope that brought healing to their lives.

Jesus says to us this first Sunday of Advent, we who need good news, that there is healing in hope. So whatever you are facing, whatever circumstances are spinning around your life, whatever difficulty you find yourself in right now, whether it's failing health, a broken relationship, a spiritual crisis, lift up your heads, live toward hope, and there find healing.

If you are looking for that hope, Jesus Christ is coming for you. He is coming to you right now. If you are not a Christian today, I urge you to open your heart and your life to Jesus. Invite Jesus to restore what is broken in you, to forgive you of sin, to heal the hurt, to be that hope to you. Begin the journey of faith at the beginning of the journey called Advent by becoming a Christian or by being a Christian becoming. And in so doing, live into hope.

Perhaps you say, "I am a Christian and have been for some time. There was a time in my life when I knew I was walking with the Lord. I was close to Christ. And yet those days seem so far away." There is good news. Lift up your heads! Jesus is coming. There is hope and healing in Christ. You can endure any "What" if you have a "Why." For the Christian, that "Why" is the One who comes, even Jesus Christ.

Blessed Virgin Mary

Greetings, favored one! The Lord is with you.
—Luke 1:28

The way we tell a story has much to do with what the story tells. Regardless of our age, hearing "once upon a time" sets us all up to hear a tale. Agatha Christie enchanted us by writing mysteries with gut-wrenching surprise endings. Sometimes, a novelist sets the tone of a work by putting an almost unbelievable surprise at the beginning (like John Grisham did in *The Testament*). The good news about Jesus Christ begins with a surprise, is told in surprising ways, and ends with history's transforming surprise, the resurrection. In a word, the gospel is surprise from beginning to end. Here is how it began.

The Roman Empire under the reign of Caesar Augustus covered the ancient world like a worn quilt on a rumpled bed. Roman occupation forces, Roman commerce, Roman culture with all its Greek baggage blanketed the Mediterranean basin. The Eagle's standard cast its shadow everywhere, even in the tiny Galilean village of Nazareth.

Nazareth was an almost insignificant bump in Galilean landscape. Nazareth, that hovel of a hamlet, was the lowest of the low of the many villages in northern Israel. In a word, Nazareth wasn't even a crossroad on the way to anywhere. Nazareth was so out of the way that any way around it was a better way. There in Nazareth, on an unexceptional day as most days were, the angel Gabriel greeted a peasant girl with words that would stick to her forever.

"Hail, thou that art highly favored. The Lord is with thee. Blessed art thou among women." Those angelic words in the King James Version set in motion a devotion to Mary that nearly parallels many Christians' devotion to Christ. Roman Catholics around the world venerate, honor, and are devoted to Mary in ways that seem strange to those of us reared in the evangelical tradition. The "Hail Mary" sounds almost like a foreign language on a Baptist's lips. "Hail Mary. The Lord is with thee. Blessed art thou among women. Blessed is the fruit of thy womb, Jesus. Holy Mary, mother of God, pray for us sinners now and in the hour of our death."

The beloved "Ave Maria" by Franz Schubert melodically holds in Latin the "Hail Mary" with exquisite beauty. Who would question the appropriateness of beginning a wedding ceremony with Schubert's "Ave Maria"? Even in Protestant precincts, most know "Ave Maria" is "Hail Mary." Interesting. Our confusion about the words cannot drown out our love for the music. Maybe we would be wise to let the music be God's invitation to meet Mary all over again. We think we know her, but do we?

In all candor, Christians outside the Catholic-Orthodox-Anglican communities read Luke's account of Mary's obedient faith and simply do not know what to do with this one God praised as the most blessed of all women for all time. We simply do not know what to do either with her or the text that speaks of her. To borrow words from Oscar Hammerstein, "How do you solve a problem like Maria?" We don't know.

On one side, many Roman Catholic believers devote their lives to Mary as the Mother of God, the *theotokos*, the "God bearer." She is venerated as the Queen of Heaven, the ever Virgin, co-redemptrix with Christ. On the evangelical side, where I find myself, we read Luke's account but avoid any hint of honoring Jesus' mother lest we be accused of being pro-Roman Catholic or worse, of being less devoted to Christ as Savior and Lord. We are really in a pickle. We either side with the Catholic position that embraces Mary as the co-redemptrix with Christ, or we go to the evangelical side of the table and simply don't talk about her. Is there a better way to celebrate this woman the Bible says is to be honored above all women?

As you might imagine, the Bible helps. In fact, Mary's devotion to God as recorded in Scripture suggests that every person is called to bear such a witness, to dare to follow Jesus in the way Mary did. What can we learn from the mother of our Lord? What can she teach us about making a difference for God in our lives in this day in which we live?

At the very least, Mary's devotion to God invites us to welcome God's "new thing" breaking into our lives. Traditional piety, as you might imagine, wraps its arms around that which tends to be old, predictable, "there." Traditional piety is the replaying of the old, living in the old, memorizing the old. You may be like me. I am a dyed-in-the-wool traditionalist. I know of only one example of contemporary architecture I like. I have tried to appreciate modern art only to leave galleries crammed with Pollacks with my feet aching and my head empty of appreciation. I am a shameless traditionalist. I enjoy and glory in things that are traditional. Even so, a traditional, pietistic relationship to God tends to savor exclusively the old.

Think of your own church. Think of what happens when the music minister introduces a new hymn in worship. The letters and comments soon follow: "Can't we sing the old songs around here anymore?" "What's wrong with the old songs?" I love the old songs. I like to sing them, hear them, even play them on the piano. I would sing "The Old Rugged Cross," "Amazing Grace," "Blessed Assurance, Jesus Is Mine," "When the Roll Is Called Up Yonder" most any Sunday. Has the thought crossed our minds that at one time, these beloved hymns were the new songs?

Has it ever occurred to anybody that "Amazing Grace"—written in the eighteenth century—was not the theme of the Pauline missionary enterprises? And yet, we wrap our lives around the old when in fact biblical piety sees the old as God's preparation for the new. We are not to live in the old; we are to learn from it and find our roots there so God can prepare us to live in and even into the new. Our very Bible is divided into what we call Old and New Testaments or covenants. In the "old," we glimpse the "new": God preparing a people for the new in Christ. And yes, the "new" in Christ is God calling us to newness day by day.

Who can forget the immortal words of the Prophet Isaiah as recorded in chapter 43 where God says, "Do not remember the former things, or consider the things of old. I am about to do a new thing; now it springs forth, do you not perceive it? I will make a way in the wilderness and rivers in the desert" (Isa 43:18-19). The Apostle Paul writing in 2 Corinthians 5:17 said, "If anyone is in Christ, there is a new creation: everything old has passed away; see, everything has become new!" And then the last book of the Bible, the Revelation, ends with God saying, "See, I am making all things new" (Rev 21:5).

Why do we struggle with cocked head and shrugged shoulder to hear, to entertain, to consider, to welcome the new? Mary could have looked at Gabriel with a jaundiced eye and said, "I like the old ways better. Go find yourself somebody else." And history would have changed, or history as we know it would not have happened at all.

The new. Who doesn't enjoy driving a new car or sporting a new haircut or moving in to a new house? Yes, when the new is something we want or an experience for which we long, rapture blinds us to risk. We pride ourselves on our new things. The new hardly goes unexpected or unwelcomed in our experience. But not always. Times are, we prefer the ruts of tradition received, the worn clichés of faith inherited, the warm blanket of songs remembered to receive much of anything new. Mary teaches us that we who follow Jesus must ever move our lives to the edge, ready for the new where God is at work making "all things new."

There is something more. God's "new" is often subversive in nature. Could you let yourself believe, just for a moment, that we worship a subversive God? Mary, rather than being the royal princess about to be married to the prince, is nothing more than a dirty-soled, callous-palmed serf. Here is the picture of God working subversively to bring about God's purposes. God is a "bottom up" God, not a "top down" God. At least with Mary—perhaps with all of us—God works subversively, behind the scenes, to bring about God's greater purposes in our lives and in history.

The Church has rarely gotten this message. We have created institutions, bureaucracies, hierarchies. We have uncritically believed this idea that God works from the top down. Not so. At least not from the place where Mary hears angel-speak. There, God works from the bottom up. God so often has and does and, I imagine, always will. God is a subversive worker. But we have trouble believing it could be so for us, much less "getting it."

Roman Catholic history in the last 150 years reveals an excellent illustration. In 1854, Pope Pius IX issued a document in which he stated as infallible doctrine of the Catholic Church that the Blessed Virgin Mary was immaculately conceived without sin. That infallible doctrine of the Roman Catholic Church today teaches the Virgin Mary was conceived in her mother's body without sin. She was born without sin so that she could bring Jesus, the sinless One, into the world. It is called the doctrine of the Immaculate Conception of the Blessed Virgin.

Almost 100 years later in 1950, Pope Pius XII declared as infallible dogma of the Church that at her death, the Blessed Virgin Mary was bodily assumed into heaven. Her body was not subject to decay. Meaning what? Meaning that when Mary died, she was bodily taken up into heaven. My purpose here is not to take issue with these twin teachings of the Church in Rome and others like them referring to Mary, although I must say that if I embraced them I would be Roman Catholic.

But note this: The Roman Catholic faithful, who have claimed to have met Mary in out-of-the-way places like Guadeloupe, Lourdes, Fatima, even Conyers, Georgia, may be saying something more about God than about Mary. God cannot be put in dogma. God cannot be enshrined in buildings or in a creed or in an institution. Rather, God is always working subversively to bring about God's higher purposes.

Who among us doesn't know a family, maybe your family, where a little child, perhaps a three-year-old, was God's subversive agent to bring the family closer to God? It wasn't that they were infidels, arrogantly ignoring God. It was, however, that little child and her innocent childlike faith, her learning the stories of Jesus, her imagining God to your heart that drew the rest of the family to God. God subversively brought them to the heart of God through the simple faith of a child.

Read the history of the human family. Time after time after time, when all hope seemed lost, God was at work in a back roads place like Nazareth to turn and change the course of history. Mary tells us that God's work is often subversive in nature. God works from the bottom up.

There is one more thing here, perhaps the riskiest of all. God is doing the new. Be ready for it. God's work is often subversive. But note this: God's subversive work is to birth Christ into the world today—right now—through us. Mary's devotion, her obedience, her willingness let God bring God's only Son into the world through her. Can we do any less? To be a Christian, a follower of Jesus Christ, is to submit to God as Mary did. God, whose power and love brings Christ into our lives, invites us to bring Christ to others through our lives.

It seems to me that to be "Marian" in our theology is not so much to venerate Mary but to find strength and encouragement from her; to let Christ be born out of our lives into the lives of others. Could this not be what Paul had in mind when he wrote to the Colossians, "Christ in you, the hope of glory"? Is this not the meaning of the new birth that Christ is born in our hearts? To be reborn by faith is, in the deepest parts of our lives, to submit to Christ created within us, and then from our lives to witness Christ's life to others. Mary is teaching us that lesson.

So how do you solve a problem like Maria? Some will continue to venerate her, and for them, that may be important, if not required. I am absolutely confident there are others in the Christian faith who will never let "Mary" pass their lips lest they be accused of being Roman Catholic sympathizers. Could we not go back to the Bible and remember that God's Word is always our sure and certain foundation? God's Word says that this woman is to be honored among all women for all generations. Why? Because she obediently submitted to God, allowing God to bring Jesus Christ into our world, Word made flesh through her physical body. Is that not what God calls us to do? God calls us to let Christ, the living Word, be born in our hearts and from our lives that people may see Christ in us. That, my friend, is what Mary continues to teach us about being Christian.

A Disturbing Favor

Do not be afraid, Mary, for you have found favor with God.
—Luke 1:30

When you visit the Orthodox Church of the Annunciation in Nazareth today, you are struck by how old the building is. The church is etched with age. The mammoth stones used to build the church show the passing of time. The large doors, weathered and splintered, almost prevent you from coming in, and yet you want to go in. You want to get in the church. When you walk in, you are met with overwhelming sensory bombardment. The noxious smell of incense that has burned there for hundreds of years teases your nostrils. There, gilded icons adorn the walls like thick draperies. In a word, you are drawn into another world when you walk into this church.

But of course you are not there today to view the church. You are there to walk through the church to the little room—really a chapel—on the other side of the church's nave. There, stone steps descend down to a place where it is believed the angel Gabriel met the Virgin Mary. In that tiny chapel, you find an old well around which the church is built. Tradition says on a certain day in a certain week in a certain year in that place, at that well, the angel Gabriel appeared to a young woman whose name was Mary. By our reckoning of years she could not have been more than fifteen or sixteen years old. It was at that well, according to tradition, that an unplanned meeting took place between an angel representing God and this peasant girl.

There is no way Mary could have anticipated Gabriel's visit. I want to believe she was going there to draw water for her family. She wasn't expecting to have her life turned upside down, but that is exactly what happened. Mary, the darling girl of Nazareth, had her whole life changed at a well one day.

Like every young girl, Mary had dreams. She was betrothed to her dream man, Joseph, the honorable carpenter of Nazareth. He was the dream man personified. Joseph, portrayed by the Gospel writer Matthew as the dreamer, is like his namesake in Genesis. He dreams. It is Joseph, according to Matthew, who receives this news in the dream as Mary received it from the angel. So the dream man is betrothed to the dream girl. They are planning their wedding when all of a sudden everything changes.

Dreams. Mary dreamed of a home. She dreamed of children. To birth and rear children was her gift of life in that culture. Children would have been the ultimate gift to her husband and to her family. Like every woman and man, she dreamed of security and safety. But all of that changed when Gabriel appeared to her at that well.

I want us to think about Mary. The text from Luke we call "The Annunciation" brims with rich meaning at Christmas. The Annunciation is a key passage in Roman Catholic theology, and quite frankly all Christians would be wise to make it central to Christian thinking and practice. I am not here today to give a detailed critique of where I agree with my Roman Catholic friends or disagree with them, but I will say to you that we in the Protestant house have missed it on Mary. In our fear of sounding or looking or even speaking like a Roman Catholic, we have so distanced ourselves from the word of God that we have done violence to a text that is so full of meaning.

Captured in a word, Mary is blessed above all women (Luke 1:26-38). Why was she chosen? In that day, there were many other Mary look-alikes in Nazareth and dozens of other Galilean villages. There were other virginal women who were fourteen and fifteen. But why this Mary? We are simply told that she found favor with God. In fact, that phrase is used twice in this text. I have read this passage so many times, and I suppose I've noticed it before, but it hit me not long ago that in verse 28 and again in verse 30, Mary is addressed as "the favored one." In fact, that is the title Gabriel gives to her. "Hail, favored one." Then two verses later Gabriel says to her, "You have found favor with God." Mary is twice favored.

The word "favor" in the text is the word from which we get the English word "grace." It is, in Greek, the word *charis*. You are the "charismatic one"; you are gifted. God's unmerited favor has come to Mary. Here is where I differ with my Roman Catholic friends. It is an honest disagreement. Mary is never referred to in this text as a sinless person, nor is it suggested that she never made a mistake. She probably, like all young girls at times, fussed at her mother. I'm sure she did. I'm sure she thought her father was terrible because he asked her to do all kinds of menial tasks around the house or keep the rules. I'm sure Mary disobeyed her parents every once in a while. The text calls her the favored one, all the while never suggesting she was perfect.

The angel says to her, "You will conceive in your womb and bear a son, and you will name him Jesus. He will be great, and will be called the Son of the Most High, and the Lord God will give to him the throne of his ancestor David" (Luke 1:31-32). As young Mary hears this, as she aborbs this, she is perplexed, troubled, and frightened. "Do not be afraid, Mary" (Luke 1:30). The word *phobos* is used in the text; our word phobia, "fear," originates from it. Gabriel's greeting is an emphatic command. Gabriel doesn't say, "Fear not," but rather, "Stop your fearing!" Why? Because everything about Mary at that moment communicated terror to the angel. Terror? Mary, you have just been told you are going to bring the Son of God into the world. Why are you so terrified? All she could think about was the fact that she was unmarried and pregnant. Her fate within months would be under a pile of stones, stoned to death as required by the law of her people.

I call this a disturbing favor. Indeed it is. To say "Yes" to God in this moment placed her in the most brutal danger. That danger, that risk, that difficulty captures my imagination. At some level of our lives when we come to the place of saying "Yes" to God, we put our lives not so much in a safe place—yes, safe with God—but rather, in human terms, a dangerous place.

You ask, "How so?" Why would saying "Yes" to grace put us in a dangerous place? This is hardly what any of us want to unwrap before Christmas. You mean that if I say "Yes" to God today, rather than luxuriating in the season, I'm going to find myself in a difficult place? My friend, hear the good news today that is first terrifying news. The good news that is first bad news suggests that when we say "Yes" to God's grace, we are saying "No" to all that is not grace, to what I would call non-grace.

Contrary to what our culture would have us believe, we don't journey with God through what I call the Christian cafeteria. The risky, dangerous side of Christian faith is not one entree in the list of things available to you, one you can take or leave. How we would like to believe that the entire Christian experience is only the dessert in the cafeteria line. You know what I mean. When you go to the cafeteria, they always march you by the desserts first. For people like me who gain weight looking at food, this is not good.

I've often threatened to my family that I would travel to a city where nobody knew me, go to a cafeteria, and load up my tray at the desserts station. Somehow we think the Christian journey is like that. We come to the dessert first, thinking that's the entire meal. We come to the place where we receive the grace of God and say, "Now I've got the goodies. Now I'm going to heaven and everything else is going to be easy." We in the Baptist house of faith have so emphasized getting saved and going to heaven that we forget all the disturbing stuff that goes with grace.

To say "Yes" to grace is to say "No" to non-grace. And what is non-grace? Non-grace is this idea that somehow we can earn our righteousness, that we can somehow be good enough for God's favor. If we go to enough church services and read enough Bible and be a "good person," whatever that means, then everything is going to be fine. Become a Christian and everything that follows in life will work out for you. This story suggests the opposite. The story says that when we become a Christian, many things may become more difficult. Frankly, life becomes more complicated because you said "Yes" to grace. Grace complicates our loyalties and our desires. Grace challenges our prejudices and questions our motives. Grace disturbs our checkbook and confronts our materialism. While grace uncomplicates our eternal destiny, grace calls from us higher duty.

And yes, we miss the outrageous favor of God if we think Mary was good enough to be the mother of our Lord. To think that God chose Mary because she was sinless or because of her righteousness—neither word mentioned in the text—diminishes the radical word of grace. For reasons known only to God, Mary simply found favor in God's eyes. For reasons unknown even to you, you too have found God's favor. Truth to tell, more grace might break out in our lives if we would simply be like Mary, open to grace. It might change our lives within. I know it would radically change our relationships with other people. Why? Because at Christmas time we want the gift of God under the Christmas tree, which is grace, eternal life, but we are so stingy about giving that grace to other people.

Here is a disturbing favor because grace is the opposite of what we have come to experience and how we behave. Yet, at Christmas, this might be the most precious gift any of us could receive. I know it would be the most precious gift you could give. Here is a disturbing favor because saying "Yes" to grace gives us a responsibility at Christmas. *Disturbing grace* gives us a duty. In a word, it requires us to live where grace takes us. The moment Mary said "Yes" to God—when she said, "Yes, I will do this. I am the Lord's servant. I will go where God takes me"—she headed to where the stream of God's grace took her.

I will never fully be able to say to a woman, "I know how it feels to be pregnant," because I am never going to have that feeling. But I have gone through three pregnancies with Kathie and have witnessed women go through pregnancies across the years. When you are carrying a child, it is a tender and dangerous time. There is a sense that when a woman conceives a child, she simply goes where the child takes her. Grace is like that. Don't miss it. When we say "Yes" to God in grace, we say "Yes" to wherever grace takes us.

In 2002, our former president, Jimmy Carter, received the Nobel Peace Prize. You can now buy his lecture. This is one of the most prestigious awards in the world, honoring people who are advocates for peace. It was given to our beloved former president, who, whether you agree with him politically or not, or whether you liked what he did when he was president or not, in my judgment is still the most Christian of leaders in the world.

Hear what President Carter said before the world when he received this prize: "The unchanging principles of life predate modern times. I worship Jesus Christ, whom we Christians consider to be the Prince of Peace. As a Jew, he taught us to cross religious boundaries in service and in love. He repeatedly embraced Roman conquerors, other Gentiles, and even the more despised Samaritans." He continued, "In order for us human beings to commit ourselves personally to the inhumanity of war, we find it necessary first to dehumanize our opponents, which is in itself a violation of the beliefs of all religions. Once we characterize our adversaries as beyond the scope of God's mercy and grace there lives lose all value. We deny personal responsibility when we plant land mines and days or years later a stranger to us, often a child, is crippled or killed. From a great distance we launch bombs or missiles with almost total impunity and never want to know the number or identity of the victims." He concludes, "War may sometimes be a necessary evil, but no matter how necessary, it is always an evil, never a good. We will not learn how to live together in peace by killing each other's children."[1]

It is to our former President's credit that in his own soul he has simply sought to live where grace took him. And yes, that can be a disturbing, dangerous place.

What is this text saying? I think it says that grace brings us to the place, disturbing though it may be, where we hold a baby in our arms. When Mary said "Yes" to God at that well, she said "No" to what was not grace and found herself flowing in the river of the grace of God, going wherever grace took her. Within months, she found herself holding a baby in her arms. Grace always takes us to Jesus.

Whatever else you may think Christmas is now or what it might be in the future, Christmas is all about Jesus. Jesus loved you and me when we were so ugly and unlovable, and we still are. Jesus comes to us with this incredible, disturbing, gracious gift of God that says, "No matter what you have done or who you think you are, God has a gift for you, and that gift is the gift of life in Jesus Christ." Yes, that does mean heaven, but it means all kinds of things before we get to heaven. It means living in risky, even dangerous ways in a world that still doesn't want to hear much about peace, that sells newspapers talking about war but is afraid to take the risky steps that lead to reconciliation and to understanding. Why? Because that might take a little more time, and we might not be in total control of the process. If we believe in this Christ, who is the Prince of Peace, we believe that he is Wonderful Counselor, Mighty God, Everlasting Father; if we believe deeply in our soul that Jesus is the answer for the deep maladies of the human family, then it seems to me we would be wise at Christmas to begin living the risky dimensions of the Christian faith. That might just require us, like Mary, to find our whole lives changed.

[1] Jimmy Carter, *The Nobel Peace Prize Lecture* (New York: Simon & Schuster, 2002), 16-20.

Magnificat

My soul magnifies the Lord.
— Luke 1:46

Can you see her? The angel has left Mary in the shadow of an awesome promise. That shadow will cast its cool and opaque cloak over her life from this moment on and as long as forever can be. Now that she has said "Yes," what happens next? Will first-blush wonder give way to stark terror? Or will Mary find a new way, a radically new response to the God who has acted in her life?

We meet two women in whose lives courage erupts like a volcano. I don't know about you, but when I think of Christmas, the words *hope, joy, glory, peace,* and the wonderful gift of *love* come to mind. But I don't often think, in fact I can't ever remember thinking, of associating Christmas with *courage.* Somehow courage is not the word of choice. Yet in the stories about Jesus' mother from the Gospel of Luke, courage breaks out of unsuspecting lives in seemingly unbelievable ways.

Get the picture. Mary is probably in her mid-teens. In that day, fathers married off their daughters in their tender teens. So Mary was probably fourteen or fifteen years old when she became engaged to Joseph. The marriage was probably arranged when Mary was a small child. The time neared when she would go to Joseph's house as his bride and become his wife and the mother of his children. Suddenly, in an unsuspecting and terrifying moment, Mary met the angel Gabriel.

I don't know how you greet Christmas. I have no way of knowing what you do with surprise visits from people at unsuspecting times. But I tell you this was not the person Mary wanted on her visitor list that day. Nevertheless, there in the town of Nazareth, Gabriel broke into her life and said to her, "Mary, you are the one who will bring God's Messiah into the world." Mary listened. She asked questions. Then we are told she responded to the angel by saying, "Let it be with me according to your word" (Luke 1:38).

Look at Mary for just a moment. Take a Kodak picture of her and you will see a person in whose life there was no security, no proof, little optimism, and the greatest "No" of all in that place, no husband. Now mind you, to be pregnant and unmarried at any age is a frightening prospect, but to be pregnant and unmarried in the first century could be terminal.

What would you have done? Mary gathered up what little bit of courage she had and traveled a great distance to visit her kinswoman, Elizabeth. Mary lived in northern Galilee; Elizabeth lived in Judea to the south. Watch Mary as she takes that long journey south, apparently by herself. Finally, she arrives at Elizabeth's house. Can you see the two women? There is Elizabeth trafficking in cold cream and memories. Quite the opposite, Mary has only recently put her dolls away and started shaving her legs. Elizabeth will be only the second woman in history to file a maternity claim against Medicare, Abraham's wife Sarah being the first. She is in her old age, six months pregnant with the child who will become John the Baptist. To her home comes her kinswoman Mary. When Mary walks into the house, the fetal John the Baptist twists, stretches, "leaps" in Elizabeth's womb.

Luke tells us that when Mary greeted Elizabeth, Elizabeth was filled with God's Spirit and broke into effusive blessings. A word not normally found in that day on a woman's lips—always on a man's—to *bless* God, to *bless* God in the company of the faithful, to offer the *blessing* to God. Elizabeth gives Mary liberal blessings. Elizabeth takes on the role of the giver of blessing to God. "Blessed are you [Mary] among women, and blessed is the fruit of your womb" (Luke 1:42). And then perhaps the greatest blessing given to Mary of all: "And blessed is she who believed that there would be a fulfillment of what was spoken to her by the Lord" (Luke 1:45). In other words, "Mary, thank you for saying a profoundly simple 'Yes.' Bless you."

After Mary hears Elizabeth's blessings, she breaks out into song:

My soul magnifies the Lord, and my spirit rejoices in God my Savior, for he has looked with favor on the lowliness of his servant. Surely, from now on all generations will call me blessed; for the Mighty One has done great things for me, and holy is his name. His mercy is for those who fear him from generation to generation. He has shown strength with his arm; he has scattered the proud in the thoughts of their hearts. He has brought down the powerful from their thrones, but has lifted up the lowly; he has filled the hungry with good things, and sent the rich away empty. He has helped his servant Israel, in remembrance of his mercy, according to the promise he made to our ancestors, to Abraham and his descendants forever. (Luke 1:46-55)

Can you see, hear, and savor the scene for a moment? Elizabeth pours rich blessings from her Spirit-filled soul; Mary breaks into jubilant song.

"My soul magnifies the Lord, and my spirit rejoices in God my Savior." In Latin, the first word is *Magnificat.* The "Magnificat"—this song of daring faith—has been set to music by composers through the ages. Major composers from Johann Sebastian Bach to John Rutter, and so many in between, have crafted music using this text.

Go to any cathedral in England today and at the Evensong service you will hear the "Magnificat" sung or spoken. It is a song of courageous faith. I wonder what you would have said? Don't miss it. Mary turns on all of the lights in her life and beams her praise toward God. If you look at the text carefully, you notice that as Mary begins this song of courageous, risky faith, she speaks of God and what God has done. The masculine noun is used throughout the text referring to God: God has done this—God has done that—God is the One who is my Savior. Mary and Elizabeth, two incredibly courageous and daring women, took their lives such as they were and beamed the light in their lives toward God.

What are these verses saying to us as we prepare to celebrate the feast of Christmas? It seems to me at the very least they are saying that God is always worthy of our praise. In many churches, the ushers return the offering plates to the altar or Lord's Supper table as the congregation stands and sings the Doxology. The Doxology says, "Praise God from whom all blessings flow." Who cannot raise his or her voice and adore God who is generous, giving, gracious? The danger, however, in singing the Doxology is that the word "all" is given definition from our own narrow perspectives. "Praise God from whom all blessings flow." What does that mean? That means my changing health, the tenuous security of my job, the blessing of my children and family, the gift of church, that which we call financial security, and so forth. Fill in your own reasons. We define "all."

This text is saying something radically different. Mary's song suggests we would be wise not only to praise God for what God has done, but to go on and simply praise God regardless. Mary's daring song is profoundly courageous: "God, my life is offered to you because you are always worthy of praise."

It has been several years since what I call the "praise God for everything" madness died. There was a moment in the Christian story back in the 1960s and early 1970s, which some may remember, when Christians were admonished to praise God for everything. I still have copies of books I purchased at that time.

The basic thesis of this movement in the Christian family was that regardless of what happens in your life, praise God for it. Your wife or your husband is diagnosed with a life-threatening illness, "Thank God for that." You lose your job, "Praise the Lord for that." Your child has some physical difficulty, "Praise God for that." Whatever happens, praise God.

One of many difficulties with this idea is the fact there is not one syllable of Scripture endorsing it. Yes, the Bible teaches us to praise God for life's blessings, wonder, and majesty. The Bible also includes the witness of Paul who said, "Give thanks in all circumstances" (1 Thess 5:18). We are admonished to praise God simply for God's God-ness. What about saying to God, "I thank you for who You are, regardless of what has happened." How many are the poor souls who snicker at grace and sneer at God because they think God did not deliver their little Santa Claus wish list to them. "God, if you don't deliver what I think is a blessing, if you don't come through for me when I need you, then you are off my list."

The Bible tells us that people of faith know God is the One always worthy of praise simply because God is God. Hear the gospel. The Christmas story, the Jesus story, the Calvary story, the empty tomb story, the whole gospel story is not a story that says God comes to us depending on whether we are naughty or nice. The Gospel tells us God comes to us because we are all naughty and broken and dying. The Apostle Paul said it this way: "While we still were sinners, Christ died for us" (Rom 5:8). God comes to us at our lowest point, at the nadir of the human story to say "I love you."

If there is any word that needs to be heard at Christmas, it is the word we could learn from Mary and the angels who said, "Praise God! My soul praises God." Christmas is the feast in which we are summoned to praise God. God is worthy of praise. God is the One from whom and in whom and to whom all of us have our very being. That is why we sing, "Joy to the world, the Lord has come." Christmas is God in human flesh. Our fore-parents of old in Appalachia help us remember a song whose writer is lost in the nameless winds of time. "What wondrous love is this, O my soul, O my soul, What wondrous love is, O my would, O my soul, this that caused the Lord of Bliss, to bear the dreadful curse for my soul." Praise God who has loved us so.

When I think of Christmas, my mind travels to places where I have lived, to rooms in which I have mused, to sounds I have heard, to spaces I have decorated. At every stop, I take in the panorama made by human hands to welcome the God-human child. So much preparation, so much "cleaning up," sprucing up to celebrate this one who comes so simply, so quietly, so beautifully. In reality, in utter humility, our Lord comes to tell us, indeed to show us that Christmas is not about our cleaning up for God's advent. Rather, Christmas is about God coming to us at the lowest point of our lives in order to make us whole. Perhaps a better preparation for Christmas would be to "uglify" our spaces to remind us of the deep, deep love of Jesus. Such daring love alone tells us God is worthy of praise.

There is something else peeking around the corners of the story. Don't miss it. This worthy-of-praise God is always at work. God doesn't take a holiday. In all our lives in all ways God is always working to bring about the kingdom of God in and through the likes of us. There is a provocative verse in this song that you may not find so provocative at first read. The more I read it, however, the dicier it gets. "[God] has helped his servant Israel, in remembrance of his mercy, according to the promise he made to our ancestors, to Abraham and to his descendants forever" (Luke 1:54-55). You say, "What is so dicey about that?" Read it. No, hear it again and remember who is singing. This is Mary's song. Listen to it. Read it one more time

Here is Mary, a young woman—an unmarried, pregnant young woman—who is in the presence of another woman, Elizabeth. Like Mary, Elizabeth has no rights apart from those granted by her father or husband. First century Jewish women were relegated to the back balcony of the synagogue. And yet Mary is the one who reminds us that God has been working through Israel and through Abraham and Isaac, Sarah and Rebekah, Jacob and David, Solomon and all the people of God throughout history. God has always been working. And now look, she says. "God is working in my life." You mean the Almighty God, who spun the world into existence, who brought a slave people out of captivity, who led them through the desert, who gave them promised land, who taught them to worship, is the very God who is now at work in the likes of an unwed mother from Nazareth? Yes! God is always at work.

Some of us have a hard time believing that at Christmas. The Christmas message whispers a shout that God is at work to bring life and glory, wonder and grace out of all of our lives. God is the one who is always at work. Is there any more needed gift at Christmas? The trinkets we unwrap under the tree and the treasures we value so much can never satisfy the need for a transformed heart made new by God who works in and through our lives.

Don't shortchange God at Christmas. Just when you think God may have abandoned you, just when you think God wants nothing to do with you any-more, God will surprise you and break into your life. At Christmas, God says, "I'm still working. Don't wrap me up and leave me looking pretty under a tree."

When we realize that God is always at work, an uncommon courage is born in our lives. Let me give you some tangible examples. Parents of adult children see this all the time. Through the twists and turns of life, you have both come to the place—parent and child, child and parent—where the hugs, the "I love yous," and the tenderness that was there when you were younger and your children were small has now gotten lost with the Christmas clutter.

Maybe this year you could revisit those tender moments by looking into the eyes of your now-adult children and saying, "I thank God that we have shared life together." You say, "I don't think I could do that with my fifty-year-old son." Or "I don't know that I could say that to my eighty-year-old mother." Perhaps Mary's example could be the Christmas gift we need most this year.

Some folks have fences to mend with a friend, a coworker, a neighbor, a fellow church member. There is no way we can share life together over years or decades and not somewhere along the journey hear the wrong thing or say the wrong thing or be hurt by someone's words. Someone expressed an opinion, made a comment, failed to make eye contact across a room; something "they" did or failed to do hurt. Maybe what you need to do this Christmas is find that brother or sister, neighbor or friend and say, "I've even forgotten what it was we differed on, but I need you and we need each other." You say, "I don't think I could do that." You may need the gift of Christmas courage.

And yes, I suspect that more than a few believe God has failed us somewhere along the time line of life. The healing didn't come when you prayed for it. The child didn't come home, life didn't go the way you wanted it. You prayed hard, even served God in the church. You did all you were "supposed to do," and yet, in your own understanding, God didn't come through. Maybe at Christmas, what you need to do is look into God's face of incarnate love in Jesus and say, "God, I've been angry at you for a long time, but I release my anger into your loving hands." You say, "I couldn't talk to God that way." Christmas courage can visit us in many ways.

If Mary and Elizabeth, with unbridled joy and embarrassing abandon—two pregnant women, one in the spring of her life and the other in mid-winter—could sing a song exalting in courage, perhaps we could as well. If these two women could embrace each other, praise God, and sing of God's magnificence under the circumstances in which they found themselves, then maybe we could, too. And yes, if we would let God give us that kind of courage, Christmas might happen for us all.

I pray it is so. I pray that somehow the flickering candles of this season will remind us that God is always at work. God is even working in your heart right now to draw you to God and to love. If you will let God do that for you, who knows, you might even wake up to Christmas.

Sermon from the Desert

*The wilderness and the dry land shall be glad,
the desert shall rejoice and blossom.*
—Isaiah 35:1

Strange as it may seem, much less strange than it sounds, the desert, the wilderness, the wasteland is the place of all places where one hears the word of God. Isaiah talked about the parched land, the desert blooming, the crocus coming to life in the desert (Isa 35:1-6). An odd prophesy, indeed. If you have been to the land of the Bible, you know that there, the desert is so dense, so deep, so barren that you would never attempt to cross it in a day or several days. The desert goes on and on and on; there is no green thing anywhere. Yet the prophet speaks good news; that when God comes, the desert will become a fertile place, a beautiful place full of flowers, dressed beautifully in life.

Then we read that interesting line from the Gospel of Luke where it says the word of God came to John, the son of Zechariah, in the desert (Luke 3:1-6). The whole story of God's redeeming humankind starts in the desert. That's where it begins. I know what more than a few of you are thinking. The story doesn't start in the desert. That's not where it begins. It all begins in Bethlehem at the manger.

And you're right . . . well, almost right. The Christmas story is about angels and wonder and shepherds. It's that warm, fuzzy feeling we get when we cozy up in a nice stable around a manger with a sleeping baby boy. You are right. The traditional Christmas story is a beginning point, but it is not the spiritual, theological beginning. The story of God coming to us in Messiah, in Jesus our Lord—in life, in humanity—starts not in the stable but in the desert.

How so? Go back and read the record. We discover this starting desert point early in the story of God's revelation. Moses is tending sheep on the backside of a desert. You can't get any more desert than the backside of the desert. He is on the far side, in dense desert when he notices high on a mountain a bush burning, but not consumed. Note it well. The desert is where Moses meets God.

The children of Israel, led out of captivity, wander in a desert for forty years—God preparing them for the promised land. In the desert, the ragtag slaves from Egypt become the people of God. The desert is the formative place. Seven hundred years later, the exiles return from captivity through the desert. That moment is background to Isaiah's message to the people who will come through the desert as they return to the land. The exiles must travel through the desert to reach home.

Even in the Gospel record, in Matthew, Mark, and Luke, we read that our Lord spent forty days and nights in the desert preparing for his ministry. After he began his ministry, Mark records that he would often retreat to "a lonely place." The better translation for those words from the original language is "a *desert* place" (Mark 1:35).

Fast-forward some years after the death and resurrection of our Lord. Saul of Tarsus, who was to become the great preacher of the early Christian movement, spent time with God—isolated time, lonely time—in the desert of Arabia (Gal 1:17). The desert is where it all begins.

Tucked into Luke's story of Christmas is an interesting reference to a desert we almost miss. Remember the moment when the angel Gabriel came to Mary the virgin and said she was to give birth to the Messiah. Can you see the astonishment in her face? Hear the sound of her voice when Gabriel gave her that incredible news. Remember Mary's first words. "How can this be? I've never known a man. How could I give birth to a child?" The angel said, "The Spirit of God will come upon you. And the One who is to be born from you will be called the Son of the Most High" (Luke 1:29-34).

The angel saw incredulity in Mary's face questioning, doubting, wondering. And so he gave her a piece of news she could check out for herself. I paraphrase: "Okay, you still don't believe me. I'll tell you what to do. Go down and visit your kinswoman, Elizabeth. In her old age you will discover she is expecting a baby." Then this small but powerful line: "This is the sixth month for her who was said to be barren" (Luke 1:35). From the barren womb of Elizabeth—the desert womb of Elizabeth—comes the life of John the Baptist. From the virgin life of

Mary comes the Son of God, Jesus Christ. The stories seem embarrassingly clear, remarkably clear, faithfully clear; the story of redemption all begins in the desert.

There is something else in these texts that we read through quickly when Dr. Luke may in fact be hooking us—playing with our minds and our imaginations. Luke, whom one theologian called "the historian," the Gospel writer so attentive to detail—begins that third chapter with these incredible lines (Luke 3:1-2):

> In the fifteenth year of the reign of Emperor Tiberius, when Pontius Pilate was governor of Judea and Herod was ruler of Galilee, and his brother Philip was ruler of the region of Iturea and Traconitis, and Lysanias was ruler of Abilene, during the high priesthood of Annas and Caiaphas, the word of God came to John, son of Zechariah in the wilderness.

In and through these lines, Luke tells us that in the political deserts of the Caesars—from Augustus, the Caesar of Jesus' birth, to Tiberius, the Caesar of Jesus' ministry—God was doing a new thing. Beyond the insipid, bureaucratic desert of Pontius Pilate and the religious deserts of the high priests Annas and Caiaphas, God was doing a new thing. Through all of those desert places and experiences in history, God was working to speak a word, to become Word made flesh, to speak a living word from the desert.

In this moment of history, we may think the affairs of our days are so neat and tidy, carefully put together. We may not know it, but all of us at some time and more than a few of us all the time may be in a desert thirsty for a word from God. How does this sermon from the desert work? Here's an illustration. Not long ago, a church member gave me an article from *Nursing Science Quarterly*. It was written by Dorothy Woods-Smith and titled, "Power and Spirituality in Polio Survivors." Being a polio survivor, I didn't go to sleep that night before I read the article. Having lived with the residual effects of polio for nearly fifty years, I read every line.

In Dr. Smith's research for this scholarly article in a journal dedicated to the training and education of nurses, she noted that in polio survivors or, in some cases, the survivors of concentration camps, ALS (Lou Gehrig's disease), or other devastating experiences in life, "traumatic events may be associated with increasing awareness of spirituality." What did she mean? She meant that as the physical life comes under assault, the spiritual life can awaken to deeper meaning.

Through the years I've heard people make comments about the tragedies of life, trying to make sense of them, trying to give interpretive words, some understanding to the awful experiences that happen to humans. Like you, I've heard trite phrases people throw together attempting to respond to tragedy: "There has to be a reason for this." I've heard that through the years. I've even said it myself when tragedy comes: "There has to be a reason for this." This statement may actually be a question: What is the cause behind this event? What could I have done to prevent the tragedy? What did I do to cause the tragedy? What in my life or in the lives of others made this happen?

Then the biggest questions: What was God doing? Where was God when this horrific thing happened" Like you, I've said it, heard it, thought it.

The Bible opens another window. Do you see it? Perhaps we are asking the "reason" question on the wrong side of the event. Rather than querying God on causality—"God, what was your reason behind this event?"—perhaps we need to ask, "God, what is your reason beyond the event?" I don't know about you, but I've not heard many answers from God to the causal question "Why?" In my experience, God is not answering many of my questions concerning causality.

Rather, what God is trying to do on the other side of tragedy is bring blossoms out of the desert. God has not necessarily created the deserts in which we find ourselves; rather, God is busy bringing life out of the deserts in which we find ourselves. There's the sermon. There has got to be a reason for it. Yes! Life can come from the event. The flower blooms; the wilderness rejoices! There is the sermon. There in the desert, when we feel the lashing heat of judgment brought about by our sin or the sin of others. There in the desert is where we can experience God. There, in a moment when perhaps totally unplanned, unanticipated, unwanted things happened that have devastated our lives, a small bloom begins to form. The great need within is to forgive people and forgive ourselves and let go of the pain. There in the desert moment, God speaks. There, if we will listen, life can blossom in the desert.

How many times in the privacy of my study have I sat with troubled souls who look at me and ask, "Preacher, what can I do with the mess in my life?" How many of us, though respectable on the outside, though communicating all kinds of Christmas love, joy, peace, and cheer on the outside, know that deep within there is some mangled mess of life we cannot fix or change? It can't be done. I would say to you, out of the faithfulness of God, that even in the desert, even in what you call a mess, God can bring life out of death if you will let God. God's work is to carpet the deserts of life with flowering glory and to carve streams of water out of the dry wilderness ground.

How many of us would say, "The desert in my life are those incomplete sentences left by death"? Death is the great desert we all must endure. We will endure it through the pain and loss of others, and one day we will endure it ourselves. The Bible clearly teaches that death, the desert that it is, is not the end but the beginning. To some extent, all of us, regardless of when death meets us in our histories, live a life of incomplete sentences. The paragraphs have not been fleshed out. The conclusion to the story has not yet been written. Even in that desert moment of death, good news comes when God says through his Son Jesus Christ, "I am the resurrection and the life. Those who believe in me, even though they die, will live, and everyone who lives and believes in me will never die" (John 11:25-26). Those moments when loss leaves us so helpless—desert moments—can be moments when we clearly hear God speak new life into our being.

How many could say that you sing hymns and try to be engaged by the experience of worship, when inside you are parched and withered by a desert place you don't quite know how to face? The loss of a job, a dream, the affection of a friend, or something else has scorched life with a fierce heat. There is some loss—some great big, vacuous hole in your life. You wonder if God will ever speak again, much less love you. Truth to tell, the desert experiences of life have the possibility, the potential, the opportunity to either be your life's defeating moment or to become your defining moment.

In your loss, your helplessness, your inability to put words and feelings together, in the numbness of your soul, everything within you would be crushed by the event. The desert would leave you for dead. When the word of God comes and says, "Good news!" let that moment be a defining moment for you. For the desert blooms and blossoms. The word of God comes to us in the desert place.

I would not want anyone to think me insensitive. I don't write the next few sentences with any motivation to insensitivity. But I say them with love and with great conviction. If you are in the desert, you may be in the best place you could ever be. Not that you would want to be there, not that you would have orchestrated the events of your life to land in some dry, seemingly God-forsaken desert of a place. Not that you would choose to be there.

But that may be the best place you could be. It could be that in the desert you finally acknowledge that you cannot save yourself. None of us, in our own power, make the desert place live. None of us can go back and redo what was a mistake, a sin, a failure, a tragedy, relive it and make it right again. None of us can do that. But the desert in which you find yourself may be the place where the word of God becomes life to you—good news to you. There, you may at last be able to hear God say through the Prophet, "Strengthen the weak hands, and make firm the feeble knees. Say to those who are of a fearful heart, 'Be strong, do not fear! Here is your God. He will come and save you'" (Isa 35:3-4).

God is ever summoning life from death. More than a few of us feel the judgment of God in our lives, perhaps because we have never come to the place of fully experiencing the redeeming love of God. For God comes in judgment not to crush us, but to redeem us, to bring life out of the desert places.

The great hymn writers of old captured the genius of this idea in the Bible and wrote lines that lift and live. Can you hear again that wonderful verse from "I Will Sing the Wondrous Story"? It says, "I was lost but Jesus found me, found the sheep that went astray, threw his loving arms around me, drew me back into His way." That's the idea at work in John Newton's immortal lines, "Amazing grace, how sweet the sound that saved a wretch like me. I once was lost but now am found, was blind but now I see." The Scriptures, the hymn writers, God's people of old are saying to us, "We cannot come to life until we first face death." We can't know paradise unless first we know the desert.

And yes, my friend, none of us can fully glory in the wonderful promise of heaven until we first gaze into the steely void of Hell only to realize that it is our destiny without God who loves us in grace.

So you're in a desert. All outward appearances suggest prosperity, paradise, success, but you know where you are. God knows where you are. Here is the good news of Jesus Christ. Until we face our lost-ness—until we face the fact that none of us can find life in and of ourselves, that we are helpless to save ourselves unless God comes and brings life—we cannot be saved. Only when that awakening to the reality of the desert occurs can we deeply hear the good news of life made new and full in Jesus the Christ.

So you find yourself in the desert. Define it in your own terms, your own experience, your own words. Hear the good news. Our God comes and says, "There is life and good news and hope. Strengthen the weak knees. Call life to those feeble hands. Stand up. God comes with life." That is the message of Advent and of Christmas. So let God give life to you today. Let God be the life-giver to you. Don't spend any more time languishing, dying, bitter and angry in the desert. God comes and God says, "I have life for you, my friend. I gave my only Son who faced the desert experience of a bloody cross so that you could know through his glorious resurrection the possibility and reality of risen life." Let that be good news to you today. Amen.

Summons to Holy Living

*You brood of vipers! Who warned you
to flee from the wrath to come?*
—Luke 3:7

When God calls a preacher, God puts in his or her heart a holy compulsion to speak the gospel through sermons. A wise would-be preacher will go to seminary. Contrary to what you may think, there are seminary classes that teach us how to prepare and deliver sermons. The formal discipline, of course, is called homiletics. Some ease through those courses; the rest of us struggle through them. All preachers learn much under the tutelage of hard knocks.

One of the lectures you hear in a preaching class—a very important lecture—has to do with establishing rapport with a congregation of worshipers. As the sermon begins, the thoughtful preacher will convey a sense of trust to the listeners. The preacher communicates believability. In a word, you offer a metaphorical hand to the congregation and say, "I like you. What we are going to talk about today may be difficult, but I'm your friend; you can trust me." It's called establishing rapport, and it's essential in order for the sermon to succeed.

The day that lecture was given at the seminary in Jerusalem, John the Baptist was homesick. How do I know that? Because he began his sermon to the congregation in the desert with these words: "You brood of vipers! Who warned you to flee from the wrath to come?" What was amazing about that opening line was the fact that people hung around and continued listening. They wanted to hear more from this preacher who called them a "brood of snakes." To make the same point, we might use other words, perhaps more winsome, less threatening. But I assure you, John defining his audience as a "brood of vipers" was not flattering to the ears of those first century Jewish listeners.

John's sermon began to develop. He continued to preach. The message came to life. Dr. Luke concludes this episode with an incredible summary. At the end of the sermon, Luke adds, "So with many other exhortations, he preached good news to the people" (Luke 3:18). I am not sure we get it. John has called his congregation a "brood of snakes," and then Dr. Luke, commenting on the sermon, writes, "He proclaimed the good news to them." I am not sure how you put words and metaphors together, but being called a snake doesn't seem to go in the same sentence as "good news," at least not in my mind.

So what might God be saying to us through these words?

Perhaps you have noticed that in the Gospel of Luke, particularly his reporting of John the Baptist's ministry, we find detail that relates to John's message and the response he received to his message. Whereas Mark and Matthew paint a two-dimensional picture of John the Baptist, more like a black-and-white photograph, Luke offers more commentary and insight into John's personality, message, and the crowd's response. In the Gospels of Mark and Matthew, John the Baptist is simply described as a man who wore camel hair, who probably smelled like a barn, and who ate grasshoppers for lunch. He had a fiery way of preaching, and people came out to hear him. That's it for John, as Mark and Matthew tell the story.

Something more is going on in the third Gospel. Dr. Luke does not give us a black-and-white photograph. Rather, the beloved physician gives us a three-dimensional sculpture. Luke gives us the gift of seeing John the Baptist, the desert preacher, from different perspectives. He allows us to move around this wonderful character in the Christmas story and see other dimensions of John rather than simply describing him as a fire-breathing, name-calling, animal skin-wearing character.

For one thing, Luke shows us the softer side of John. Luke wants us to know that whatever else we may have heard about the desert prophet, John wasn't as harsh as some would have us think. In fact, John's sermons were so engaging that the people asked him questions. Today, we would call it dialogical preaching. The people talked back to him. Did you hear their questions?

In Luke 3:10-14, they asked, "What then should we do?" He replied, "Whoever has two coats must share with anyone who has none; and whoever has food must do likewise." Even tax collectors came to be baptized. "Teacher, what should we do?" John said to them, "Collect no more than the amount prescribed for you." Notice he didn't say, "Shut down the IRS," but rather, "Don't take more than you are supposed to collect." Soldiers also asked him, "And we, what should we do?" He said to them, "Do not extort money from anyone by threats or false accusation, and be satisfied with your wages." Are you hearing the same thing I am hearing? The "brood of vipers" sermon pulled questions from the people.

On the threshold of Christmas, we have questions, too. Our questions might sound like this: If God is coming, if God is moving toward us, if God is on the way to this place—to our lives, to our time, our history—if God is coming this way, what should we do? How can we prepare our lives so that we would be a people ready for God? What does it mean to live a holy life, and if we could do that, would it make us ready for the coming of God in Jesus Christ?

John says, "Yes, there is something you can do." Like a skilled archer, John puts an arrow in his bow and fires that arrow right into the hearts of a congregation of worshipers. He says there is something we can do. In fact, there is something we must do. This is a hard word for us to hear on the eve of Christmas. But hear it we must.

He says what we must do is confess the sin of presumptuous religion. We don't like the word *confess*. We don't warm to confession. We do not like admitting that we have failed God, others, and ourselves. We have created many euphemisms for sin. We no longer look into the mirror and say, "You sinner!" We now look into the mirror and say, "You exercised poor judgment." I don't know if you have noticed it or not, but football teams no longer lose games. They simply don't play up to their potential. We have taken confession, this seemingly harsh word, the stark word of the gospel that says "admit your sin and agree with God that you have fallen short," and, unapologetically, we have domesticated it. Call it presumptuous religion: twisting the hard words we need to hear into soft syllables, easy on our ears.

I don't know if you have noticed it or not, but it is not by accident that choirs and clergy wear purple stoles and we light purple candles during Advent. Purple is the penitential color. Those who come from more liturgical backgrounds know that in the seasons of Advent and Lent, the clergy and choir wear purple. Why? Because purple is the color signifying penance, contrition, preparation, honesty before God.

Long ago, our foreparents said the four weeks prior to the celebration of the birth of Jesus is a time when we would be wise to face our lives, ourselves, our sin, our brokenness. Why? So we could prepare for the coming of Christ. The gospel message here is a hard message. Sin is a tenured reality turned loose among us as we worship and pray, give and serve. Simply put, sin can be identified as an idea, a belief that because we are performing religious acts, because we worship in a church, sing the hymns, love the Bible, prepare for Christ's coming, we have

God in our back pockets. John knew that. He read the people's faces. "Don't begin to say to yourselves, 'We have Abraham as our father.' Or for that matter be offended, asking, 'Why are you preaching to us? We can give you our pedigree. We can trace our faith heritage all the way back to Abraham, Isaac, Jacob, Moses, David, Solomon, and others'" (Luke 3:8).

In church on Sunday morning, we can fall prey to that. Our pedigree may look impeccable. In our personal lineage, there may be a long history of faithful parents, grandparents, and great-grandparents, maybe even a preacher, a missionary, maybe two. You may be able to look back on your history and say, "All these years I've been faithful to God. What's all of this to me today?" The gospel is saying, "Beware. Confess the sin of presumptuous religion." Don't think that just because you've got the ritual down, you are ready for the Christ.

John said as much. "I baptize you with water." He meant, I perform a religious ritual for you to get you ready. "I baptize you with water, but one who is mightier than I, one that I am not worthy to stoop down and untie the thong of his sandal; he is coming after me. He will baptize you with Holy Spirit and with fire" (Luke 3:16). Such a Holy Spirit/fire baptism is the work of God in our lives preparing us for the coming of Christ. In this season adorned in purple, God comes among us in Holy Spirit fire and says, "Confess, prepare, get ready, wake up!"

I wonder if God is as impressed with our worship ritual and Sunday best as we are? The psalmist believed the sacrifices acceptable to God are a broken spirit and a contrite heart. Religion can buttress our faith, but it can never substitute for a living relationship with the living God. Presumptuous religion, even well done, is a poor substitute for honest confession.

Then John says one more thing. Put your faith to work. "If you have two tunics, give to the person who doesn't have one. And if you have food do the same." The tax collectors piped up. They were not a group of people to whom the Jews warmed, but they piped up and asked, "What are we supposed to do?" He answered, "Only take what is right. Be a person of integrity." Then the soldiers asked, "What are we to do?" John said, "Don't extort money, don't abuse people, be content with your pay." What John is saying to us is this: surprise others with the kinds of sacrifices you make. You might even surprise yourself.

Isn't it true that when we give of ourselves, when we step away from our comfort zones, go to the edge of the envelope, and do a bit beyond what we think we could do or might do or should do, we surprise ourselves? When we move out to that edge, we often realize, "I don't believe I did that." But we did.

A few years ago, the church I served as pastor became involved in a ministry to the homeless called "Interfaith Hospitality Network" (IHN). It's an audacious idea: thirteen churches in the community of different denominations, different expressions of worship came together for one sole purpose—to house homeless families. This ministry has required more than one thousand volunteers in the thirteen churches. Such a ministry always requires much from us. Yes, it has required sacrifice. Dozens of our members got involved in IHN by bringing meals to the church, being at the church throughout the night as hosts and hostesses for families, helping network adults with employment, housing, and childcare for children. IHN is but one ministry that calls believers to put their faith to work.

What is often easy in such a ministry is to volunteer to bring meals or open our checkbooks and give money, perhaps to stop by and tutor the children. What is more difficult for us is to move out of our comfort zones to sacrifice our own way of life for a night a year or two nights a year, to bunk down at the church house with a family who needs community. Interfaith Hospitality Network is only one way we put our faith to work.

Perhaps the surprising sign of an Advent season is your discovery that in actually putting your faith to work, there is a sense of wonder and enthusiasm in your life you didn't know was there. One troubling problem today is that we think like the people of old that the ritual of religion—baptism, penance, making sacrifices at the temple, going through all of the religious motions—makes us holy. In fact, what makes us a holy and prepared people is the sacrifice of ourselves.

I'm told that among our Orthodox Jewish friends in faith there is a belief that if all Israel could say at one time the Shema—"Hear, O Israel, the Lord our God, the Lord is One"—the Messiah would come. Some Jews believe that. I'm told there are Catholics who believe that if all Catholics would pray at once the "Hail Mary"—"Hail Mary, full of grace, the Lord is with thee. Blessed are thou among women. Blessed is the fruit of thy womb, Jesus. Holy Mary, mother of God, pray for us sinners now and in the hour of our death"—Christ would come. Those are wonderful thoughts. Those are dreams worthy of dreaming.

The Advent message is something different. If you want to see the kingdom of God come in your lifetime, put your faith to work. Move out of the comfort zone of your self-made security and your self-defined lifestyle where everything is carefully managed and held close, and risk something for God. It may be in the life of a single-parent child. It may be in the life of a homeless family. It may be pushing the envelope outside your comfort zone to do something for others that they cannot do for themselves. You might be surprised by the sacrifices you make.

I have thought for a long time that one of the reasons we have little is because we give little. We give little of ourselves—our affections, our affirmations, our treasures, our dreams. And yet what the gospel calls us to do is look at what we have, then look out to those who have little or nothing. As we look there and actually live into what we see, we discover what it means to be a holy people. George MacDonald, great preacher and Christian mystic of another generation, penned a sentence that is right on target: "The love of our neighbor is the only door out of the dungeon of self."

Why is it that when the room has been decorated, the carols sung, Christmas experienced, the dinner served, the presents opened, things wadded up to be thrown away, and the day is done, we wake up the next morning and wonder what happened and why? God calls us to live sacrificially in every season of the year, that who we are under God in Christ might live in grace into the lives of others for Jesus' sake.

Mother Teresa penned what she called "The Simple Path." "The fruit of silence is prayer. The fruit of prayer is faith. The fruit of faith is love. The fruit of love is service. The fruit of service is peace."[1] Who among us today would not give all that we are to wake up Christmas morning and have some of that blessed, soul-satisfying peace? Mother Teresa tells us how to find it. She says the fruit of silence is prayer. And the fruit of prayer is faith. And the fruit of faith is love. And the fruit of love is service (giving, sacrificial service). And the fruit of service is peace.

The third Sunday in Advent is the Sunday we light the pink candle. In many churches, this pink candle is called the "Joy" candle. In our church—at least for one year—we called the pink candle the Candle of Sacrifice. How do we get from Joy to Sacrifice? Here's the secret: joy is wrapped inside sacrifice. John the Baptist said as much: "If you have two tunics, give to someone who has none. Don't take more than you are required. Don't extort money. Don't abuse people. Be content with who you are." Put your faith to work. How? "The fruit of silence is prayer. The fruit of prayer is faith. The fruit of faith is love. The fruit of love is service. The fruit of service is peace." Teresa, forgive me, but the fruit of peace is joy. Such Advent truth is God's summons to holy living. Amen.

[1] Mother Teresa, *The Simple Path* (New York: Ballantine Books, 1995), 1.

Christmas Is for Children

*Therefore, the LORD himself will give you a sign.
Look, the young woman is with child and shall
bear a son, and shall name him Immanuel.*
—Isaiah 7:14

Christmas is for children. It always has been. In the eighth century before our Lord's birth, the Assyrians were the fierce warrior-nation of the Middle East. The Assyrians held all their foes in the treacherous grip of murder. The Assyrians brought their army south toward Judah. They stopped off at the northern kingdom of Israel to make a political, military arrangement. The northern kingdom of Israel and the southern kingdom of Judah, though they were of the same stock, were not of the same spirit. So the Assyrians made a pact with the northern tribe of Israel and together the king of Israel and the king of Assyria came down and surrounded the city of Jerusalem around the year 722 BC.

Everyone in the city slept restlessly with the Assyrians outside the gate, especially the king. The prophet Isaiah says of this moment in history that "the heart of [Ahaz's] people shook as the trees of the forest shake before the wind" (Isa 7:2). I say again, when the Assyrians came, everybody shook. The Assyrians were not to be trifled with. Their fierce army was at the gate. Ahaz the king, anxious and afraid, met the prophet Isaiah secretly in a tunnel under the south wall of the city. God told the prophet to take with him to that meeting his son, whose name was Shear-jeshub, meaning, in Hebrew, "A remnant shall return." Forget his name if you must, but never forget its meaning—"a remnant shall return."

There, under the city, in a dark, damp, foreboding tunnel, we meet the king, the prophet, and the boy whose name was "A remnant shall return." "Don't be afraid, my king. These two armies are but smoldering firebrands soon to be snuffed out." As the prophet speaks, "A remnant shall return" stands there silently. The child is simply there.

The prophet's words are not convincing the king. The prophet sees in his king this troubled spirit, this uncertainty, this fear. He says to him, "Ask God for a sign. God will give you a sign." The king says, "No, I'm not going to do it." "Well, the Lord will give you a sign. A young woman is with child and shall bear a son and shall call him 'God is with us.'" In that moment, as the prophet spoke the words—"A young woman is with child and will bear a son"—God was showing us long before the events in Bethlehem that Christmas is for children.

Come forward with me more than seven hundred years. Luke tells us at the beginning of his Gospel that Zechariah and Elizabeth, in their old age, on Medicare, will have a child. Mary, in her teenage years, hears news of her pregnancy, which she welcomes as being of God. Babies fill the stories at the beginning of the third Gospel. Now, from the Gospel of Matthew we meet Joseph—calculating, proud, rational, moral, righteous. He hears the news that Mary is pregnant. He has had no relations with her. He is troubled. He considers putting her away, covering the shame. Maybe he is protecting her, but assuredly he is protecting his own reputation. The angel Gabriel interrupts his plans. Gabriel meets with Joseph and says to him, "Joseph, at the center of the being of God working in history is a child." It is still so. At the center of the gospel of God coming to us in saving love is a child. Christmas is for children. It always has been.

"'Twas the night before Christmas, when all through the house not a creature was stirring, not even a mouse; The stockings were hung by the chimney with care, in hopes that St. Nicholas soon would be there. The children were nestled all snug in their beds while visions of sugar plums danced in their heads." What would Christmas be without children? Nothing! Zero! Christmas is for children.

What in the world is God saying to us in this cluster of Advent time just before Christmas? Did you hear the Bible? Did you hear it in your soul? The word is like a sharpened arrow through all of our hearts before Christmas, a word from God.

For one thing, life always has its external threats. They come at times unexpected, and often undeserved. Sometimes they come and we know they are coming. Life always has its external threats. In the eighth century it was the Assyrians. Before the dawn of the first century it was this troubling news to Joseph. In all of life—in your life and in mine—there are always external threats.

It could be health. It could be the reordering of a relationship. It could be imagined fear about the future. But all of them have Assyria as their origin.

Often we experience the external threat, we keenly observe it, but we poorly interpret it. John Claypool, quoting an imminent psychologist, is fond of saying that "Children are keen observers but they are poor interpreters." It is so for us big children, too. When the Assyrians show up, when life's external threats come to us, we keenly observe what is going on but we often misinterpret what is happening.

This phenomenon is going on right now as the Christmas story weaves its wonder into our souls. Life by definition will always have external threats. You say, "I don't know what that would be. Things couldn't be much better for me today." Just wait. There will be a call in the night. There is the opening of a door and the physician walks in the exam room. There is a closing of a door and a child walks out. Just wait. Life by definition always has its external threats, and every one of them traces its genesis to Assyria.

This is the struggle in Joseph's life. Ahaz and Joseph both struggle with this external threat phenomenon. Did you know that Joseph had Ahaz's DNA? We find this in the first seventeen verses of Matthew 1 (especially Matt 1:9). Joseph is a descendant of Ahaz. The ancient king's DNA is in Joseph. Do you see it? So Joseph comes to the moment with the DNA of Ahaz. He deals with the issue of threat so much like his foreparent. Truth to tell, you and I are of that same line. Life, by definition, always has its external threats.

What is this text saying to us? Every child is a living sermon to us in every moment of life. This child's name was "A remnant shall return." What does your name mean? What does the child's name—the presence of a child—mean in your family? What does the child mean in and to your church? What does the child's name mean in your community? Children are living sermons. Their openness to wonder, their transparent and generous affection, their visionary attitude, their incredible optimism about life all convey the word of God to us if we will listen.

Every once in a while I have the privilege of receiving one of the most priceless works of art ever created. They are all original works, and I happen to be the recipient. Often, one of these works comes to me at the close of service, when very proudly, a child who has patiently waited in line comes to me, looks up, and hands me her drawing. I'm sure she did not get the complexities of the theology in the text. I'm convinced she was not really tuned in to the meaning for our adult lives in the sermon. But she watched it all—she observed it all—and now she reminds me that in our midst are these gifts from God. If we will listen to them, we may journey with them and even because of them. "A remnant shall return." Christmas is for children. They are among us. Perhaps our need is not so much to silence them as it is to release them, to let them come alive, to honor them, to guide them, and to let them guide us. Children are living sermons in our midst.

What is the text saying to us? Don't miss it. God comes as a child. God does not come to us as rational argument nor as propositional truth. God does not come as theological system or sacred law, neither as developed mind nor sophisticated adult. No, the Almighty God who loves us so much comes among us as a child. In another text, this same Prophet says, "And a little child shall lead them" (Isa 11:6).

We are so sophisticated, so erudite in our delineation of the theology once delivered to the saints. Go to any library and cast your eyes on the reasonings of men and women across the centuries. We have made the simple complex. We have made what is innocent almost virulent. We have taken the simple gospel of Jesus Christ and made it so difficult. If you boil it all down to simple sentences, and by the way, you have to boil it down to simple sentences, God comes to us as a child and loves us unconditionally as a child. Christmas is for children. It always has been.

One more thing. God comes as a child clothed in human flesh, robed in our humanity. God comes not as a metaphorical child or an abstract child, not an imaginary child or a child in thought, but up close, a child in our midst. God comes as a child, as a person: innocent, vulnerable, open, growing, engaging, maturing, relating. God comes as a person. John said, "And the word became flesh and lived among us, full of grace and truth" (John 1:14).

God comes as a child, in the full personhood of a child. God comes as a newborn babe. So "What child is this who laid to rest on Mary's lap is sleeping, whom angels greet with anthems sweet while shepherds' watch are keeping? This, this is Christ the king whom shepherds guard and angels sing. Haste, haste to bring him laud, the babe, the son of Mary." God comes as a child, as a person, a real, living person.

What do we do with this child at Christmas? What do we do with Christmas? We have options. It is one of the wonderful things about the human species. We have options. One of our options is that we can go on with our tangled systems of reason, thought, and demanding rigor. We can continue down the road of being obtuse and complex. That is an option. Many take it. A second option is relational. We can continue to build walls that keep people out. We can write rules that make us feel righteous when we conform or guilty when we fail. We can flex our muscles and keep our arms rigid, fending off any and maybe all who would dare get too close. Yes, that is an option. We do that kind of thing well and often.

It seems that we can do something else. The text gives us another option. We can hear the good news. We can hear it beyond our ears. We can hear it beyond our minds. We can hear it down deep in our being. What is that good news? The good news is this: Ahaz, stop listening to the army marching; Ahaz, listen and you will hear a baby crying. Now, O king, you have a choice: to turn your ear to the army marching or tune your ear to the baby crying. We have the same choice. Our choice is either to listen to the Assyrians or listen to the child.

We have another choice. This other option is that we can decide to go on with our lives as we were. We can stay in our roles. We can live as adults with everything worked out: who's in, who's out, who's right, who's wrong, who's orthodox, who's heretic, who's good, who's bad, who's deserving, who's undeserving. Or we can come as a child.

An amazing transformation occurs in our lives over these Christmas days. If you have never thought about it or reflected upon it, I invite you to observe with me what happens between December 25 and January 1. I call it an amazing transformation. In this moment of wonder, having welcomed the Christ child once again into our midst, we are transformed from expectant, wonder-filled, wanting, hungry, needy children to frantic, post-Christmas, sale-agitated, fretful New Year's Eve adults. It happens in about three days somewhere between December 25 and January 1. The child disappears. All that was wonder and magic is wadded up and thrown away with the crumpled wrapping paper from Christmas morning. Poof! Gone.

What will you do this year with God who comes to you as a child? God says, "Ahaz, Joseph. I know you can make plans. I know you have your fears. I know what you have outside your gate. I know what you are thinking about the news you heard, but throw it down and be as a child. For unless you become as a child you will never, ever come to Christmas, much less Easter or the kingdom of God."

Christmas is for children. It always has been. Will Christmas be for you?

Teach Us to Pray

Call God "Father"

A number of years ago, I stood on a hillside above the little fishing village of Capernaum on the north side of the Sea of Galilee. At that site sits a church built by, of all people, Mussolini. Though none of our motives are pure, it would appear he had the church built more as a monument to himself than to remember the place where our Lord gave the Sermon on the Mount. This beautiful place is the traditional site where Jesus preached the most troubling and engaging sermon human ears have heard.

I always find it ironic to stand outside that church and look inside. Though the Sermon on the Mount is without question the greatest sermon ever uttered, the person who built the church to commemorate the Sermon on the Mount is anything but a character in history we would honor or revere.

Nevertheless, it was at that site or, if not there, a place very near there where Jesus gave the Sermon on the Mount. At the center of Matthew 5, 6, and 7, almost as if it were the fulcrum on which the entire sermon functions, is the passage of Scripture we call the Model Prayer (Matt 6:9-13). Often called "The Lord's Prayer" (with you, I can hear the organ swelling with Albert Hay Mallott's beautiful tune), these lines teach us how to pray even as they are surrounded by our Lord's more extensive teaching on prayer (Matt 6:5-15).

Let's look at a couple of things to get us started. First, the Model Prayer in Matthew 6 is in the middle of the Sermon on the Mount. I don't know what that means to you, but textually, no passage of Scripture can be understood in isolation from that which is around it. In order to interpret adequately a biblical text, we must place it in its larger context. What is its local address in a particular book (in this case Matthew)? How does this text function in the unique part of the Bible in which we find it (a Gospel)? And finally, where is this text in reference to the Bible as a whole (the New Testament)? Careful biblical interpretation requires us to explicate verses contextually.

In my judgment, it is not accidental that the prayer is placed at the center of the Sermon on the Mount. Why? Because our relationships with people cannot be separated from our relationship to God. We cannot have a right relationship to God if our relationship with others is not right. We can come to the church, pray, give, sing, even do good work for God, but if our relationship with our brothers and sisters is broken, dysfunctional, bruised, then our prayer life is obviously going to be affected. The two go together. Our relationships with God and with others are part of a whole.

The second thing I call attention to is this: when Jesus taught the Model Prayer, he made a grand assumption. Jesus believed that those who followed him would be people of prayer. Notice the text. Jesus did not say, "If you pray . . . ." Rather, Jesus said, "When you pray . . . ." The assumption is that we who are citizens of the kingdom of God—we who make up the family of faith—will be people of prayer.

Notice now what I call Jesus' two rules for prayer. First of all, talk to God; commune with God. Notice he tells us to go to the secret place, the private place (Matt 6:6). This admonition does not exclude public prayers. Some read this passage and box themselves in. "You should never offer a prayer in a church service or pray in public because Jesus said 'When you pray, go to your closet.'" When Jesus said go to your closet and pray, he wasn't saying, "Don't pray in public." He was saying, let your prayer in private be the focus of your prayer life. If you please, our public prayers are to be the overflow of private prayer. Sad indeed is the person whose only prayer is the occasional obligatory blessing at a meal. Jesus taught us in these lines that prayer is talking to God, not talking so that other people can take notes on what we are saying. Prayer is a conversation, a communion with God.

Then notice a second command. Not only are we to commune with God in prayer, but we are also to encounter God in prayer. Prayer is to be an encounter with God, not just a dialogue or a conversation addressed to God. Prayer is a relationship in which we encounter God in wonder, love, and praise. I understand Jesus to be saying that when we pray, we need to remember that prayer is more relationship than rhetoric. My journey with God in prayer has taken many turns in the course of my Christian experience. Only recently have I begun to find nourishing strength in simply being in the presence of God, aware that, to borrow Paul's borrowed line, we "live and move and have our being" in God (Acts 17:28). There is a "being with" reality that words cannot duplicate.

Truth to tell, if you had to choose between prayers of words and prayers of silence, if you had to make the choice, I would want you to choose silence over words. Why? Because in the Scriptures, we learn that the Holy Spirit knows our hearts, the Holy Spirit knows the words. What the Holy Spirit longs for in us is a relationship with God. Examples from daily life abound. To experience another as husband or wife is to know that person in a relationship that calls from us our entire being. More than words, dialogue, conversation over coffee in the morning, a marriage calls from us our entire being. And what parent does not delight in simply being in the same room with her child? So it is in our relationship to God through the experience of prayer. Being with God, cherishing God's presence, listening for God's "still, small voice," dwarf any words we could fashion in speaking to God.

The other thing encountering God is that we are wise to remember that it is not so much our physical posture as our spiritual posture. When you go the Western Wall in Jerusalem, you will see Orthodox Jews in prayer. We have mistakenly called this place of prayer "the wailing wall." Orthodox Jews moving as they pray is a posture hardwired to Jewish piety. It gives the outsider an impression of wailing or weeping, but that is not what is taking place. The Talmud says the person is to pray with all his or her body; all of his or her being is to be in the posture of prayer before God. In other words, prayer is to engage our whole being. Jesus is saying that here. Not that you and I need to do as the Orthodox do in our prayer, but that our whole being is to encounter God as we pray.

Let's now move to the content of this most beloved prayer in the Bible. Jesus said, "Pray in this way," remembering that prayer not only involves the horizontal but also the vertical. Remember that prayer is assumed in our lives, that prayer is a conversation with God, an encounter with God, then Jesus said this about prayer: "When you pray, pray in this manner." For now, I'm drawn to the first phrase, "Our Father in heaven, hallowed be your name."

The interpretation of these words is so simple and yet so utterly profound. Think with me for a few moments about how these two opening phrases mutually interpret each other. The first phrase haunts me. I have thought and rethought, said and resaid this line numerous times. "Our Father in heaven, hallowed be Thy name." The first phrase—"Our Father in heaven"—interprets the second—"hallowed be Thy name." And yes, the second phrase interprets the first. It is simple because these two phrases mutually interpret each other. There is a profound simplicity in this salutation. It's profound because here we find the key to the entire experience of prayer. Prayer's very foundation is found in these eight words: "Our Father in heaven, hallowed be Your name."

Let's unpack the first phrase. Think about the first word, "our." "Our Father." Not my Father, not your Father, but *our* Father. No authentic, meaningful prayer is purely private. I know what Matthew 6:6 says: "Go to the private place and there seek your heavenly Father." That admonition must be read in the context of the Model Prayer. Simply said, Jesus tells us that when we pray there must be the awareness, even the spiritual sense, that there are others with us. The opening words are "Our Father."

There is community in the word "our," suggesting that, though unseen, others are with me when I pray. I am not alone. Memories of their personalities, words, faces, voices, gestures all come to mind as we pray. Community is such a lovely word. All of us live as recipients of gifts we do not deserve, of friendships we cannot earn, of love we deeply need. Community. Anytime we pray the Model Prayer—whether privately or in corporate worship—we invoke others with the first word "our."

Not long ago, I stood in the Garden Tomb in Jerusalem and shared communion with the group I was leading. We had traveled together for more than a week. In that short time, we had become close friends. At this service in the Garden, others joined us for communion. Frankly, I didn't know most of the people sitting before me that day outside the old city of Jerusalem. Some were from Georgia where I live; others were from Florida, North Carolina, and Kentucky. A simple communion service brought us to the place where we sat together for worship. But when we prayed together the Model Prayer, we instantly became a community of faith. Why? Because our first word was "Our."

To our human shame, a host of evil has been done in the name of God and even in the name of prayer by forgetting that simple, inclusive word "Our." When you and I pray, we are to remember that we are not radical individualists in the family of God. We are woven into the fabric of every life that claims God as Father and Christ as Lord. It's not "my will" any more than it's what I want. Rather, we pray seeking that which will bring glory to "Our Father."

There's more here. Not only is there community in that simple word, there is also destiny. To pray the Model Prayer is not only to embrace community with your brothers and sisters of faith, but it is also to say you share a common destiny with them. We are going to be family for a long, long time. We are a part of each other's being for all eternity. The next time you attend a worship service—perhaps at your church—look around you and remember the people sitting in that space with you who have made some impact on your life. Perhaps you see a beloved Sunday school teacher from childhood, a senior adult who taught you to sing your first hymn, a beloved deacon who visited you in the hospital. All these and scores of others unseen are all sitting in your soul as you worship. The prayer's first word is "Our."

Then look at the word "Father." "Father" communicates two powerful realities. It is unfortunate so many are hung up on gender issues. I hope you will put that out of your mind for a moment. Jesus is not suggesting that God is male. Such an idea is found neither in the teaching of our Lord nor in the grand scope of biblical witness. Rather, "Father" speaks of a relationship with God who is like a caring, loving, guiding, nurturing father. Jesus used the Aramaic word "Abba" for father. It is the term of endearment meaning "Daddy." You can go through Jerusalem today and hear little children calling their fathers "Abba, Abba, Abba." They are saying "Daddy." It is a term of endearment.

This word Father reveals an intimacy with God that is far beyond a gender issue. It transcends gender; it's greater than gender. Father communicates at least two powerful realities. It says first of all that God's role in our lives is to be the role of a guide. God is a loving, faithful, fatherly guide. God is a partner with us. God is faithful to us as our guide. God is the One who never abandons us on the journey of life, even when life gets difficult. Jesus said, "I am with you always." That is the picture of God. God is the faithful father, a trusted guide.

Calling God "Father" also suggests that our relationship to God is built on trust. I don't know about the home in which you grew up, but I know that in my home, I could trust my father. I've known my dad in many different dimensions of his personality. To be sure, there are whole dimensions of his life that I will never know. But in my experience growing up in our home, I knew my father to be someone I could trust. When he gave his word I knew I could trust his word. When he said, "I'll do something," I knew he would do it. When he said, "I can't do something," I knew he couldn't do it. He might have wanted to, but I knew he couldn't. Jesus is teaching us that when we pray "Our Father," we are speaking of God in terms of a guiding, trusting relationship.

The next words—"in heaven "—lift our prayer vertically, reminding us that we are in relationship with Otherness, the Divine, the Eternal Being in whose life we have life and in whose presence we have hope. It's not arbitrary that we use the phrase "Look up!" to encourage people who are discouraged. "Set your sights high" is another expression that encourages people to look with hope to the future. When Jesus taught us to pray saying "Our Father in heaven," he was encouraging us to lift our spiritual shoulders and set our spiritual eyes on God who is both above us and with us, beneath us and around us. "Heaven" in Jesus' teaching was not so much a place—streets of gold, pearly gates, opulent mansions—as it was a metaphor for the habitation of God, the Ultimate Mystery who is radical Otherness. When we pray, we address God as Father whose Being is lovingly above us and yet intimately with us.

We press on, remembering the second phrase interprets the first and the first interprets the second. "Hallowed be your name." How do we hallow the name of God? That phrase might also be translated from the original language, "May your name be held in reverence" or "Sanctify your name." This harkens back to the third commandment from Exodus 20:7 where, in the words of the King James Version, "You shall not take the name of the LORD your God in vain." The New International Version better translates it, "You shall not misuse the name of the LORD your God." "Our Father in heaven" is paired with "Hallowed be your name." What does that mean? It means we are to live in such reverence toward God that we don't misuse our Father's name. Prayer is communion with God. Prayer is communion with a holy, righteous God, a God who is other than us. We are to honor, to sanctify God's name.

Religious Jews today do not write the word *God.* They won't do it. When I was teaching at the University of Alabama, I received papers back from my students and started noticing my Jewish students spelled God's name "G-d." I kept looking at that and asked myself, "What's going on?" Then it suddenly hit me. These were men and women who had been taught to revere the name of God. They would not write the name of God. They spelled God's name G-d.

Do you see it? The Model Prayer calls us, forces us if you please, to face what I call the casualization of spirituality that can eventuate in the trivialization of God and the cheapening of life. If you pray this prayer, if you order your prayer life around the Model Prayer, you will come into a relationship with God that sees God as holy, apart from, other than you. God is above you, beyond you, and yet God is Father, lovingly drawing you into relationship. God is above us, but God is also nearer to us than our next breath. God is "Our Father."

I marvel at people who tell me they pray for parking places or they pray before athletic contests or for good grades in school or for a date with a certain someone. I don't mean to be cross and I surely don't mean to be offensive, but when you and I take the Model Prayer seriously, we may discover that God has far more important items on God's agenda than whether or not we park close to the front door of the grocery store. In fact, God's real desire might be for us to park at the back of the parking lot so that we can have a quiet walk into the grocery store and spend a little time with God on the way. Or, God might want us to park all the way at the other end of the parking lot so that someone who is disabled might be able to park closer to the door.

When you and I pray the Model Prayer seriously, if we study these words carefully, we are drawn into the reality of God who is above, beyond, and yet nearer to us than anything we can imagine. To pray this prayer, to speak it, to experience it is to meet God and to place our lives in the grip of God.

Fifteen years ago, Kathie and I found a ridiculously cheap airfare and decided on a lark to go to London. I will never forget walking into Westminster Abbey that first time. I looked all around me and saw people from every part of the world. Standing in the magnificent house of worship were Asians, Africans, Latin Americans, North Americans, and Europeans. I saw people with skin the color of my own; I saw people with varying shades of other colors. In that church, where so much history has taken place, I'll never forget a very special moment. A priest went up into the pulpit of that church, turned on the microphone, got our attention, and reminded all of us that the great church in which we stood was not a tourist attraction but a house of worship.

Then he asked us all, "Would you join me as we pray together the Lord's Prayer?" And in that moment a reality came over me, which, at the time, seemed like a taste of heaven. People of every language and Christian tradition and experience of faith suddenly became the family of God as we prayed "Our Father."

May the praying of this prayer—the Model Prayer—be such an experience for you of wonder, community, worship, and more. When you pray, say "Our Father."

Prayer
Loving heavenly Father, we are so blessed to call you Father. Your love for us protects and guides us unlike any human parent. Though unworthy of your care, we receive uncommon grace day after day. You never give up on us, choosing to call us your children. You offer us your very life.

As time moves us on, we need your divine wisdom. Forgive us when we act more like spoiled preschoolers, demanding our way and having spiritual temper tantrums when we don't get it. Remind us when we sit before broken bread and a shared cup, that we are your children. Across our lives is the shadow of a cross and the reality of the empty tomb. Move so lovingly and so profoundly in our lives that we will grow beyond infantile immaturity to become the responsible and giving sons and daughters of God you have called us to be.

In these moments of worship, place your fatherly hand upon us all. Calm those who are afraid; comfort your children who are grieving; call anew your sons who are proud and your daughters who are selfish. Make of us, many that we are, your family today that we may rightly call you Father and faithfully be your children. This we pray through Jesus Christ, who told us and who showed us you are our Father. Amen.

From Here to Kingdom Come

*Your Kingdom come, your will be done,
on earth as it is in heaven.*
—Matthew 6:10

I think it is marvelously coincidental or providential that so many events coalesce around the third weekend in January. Children's Day is an opportunity to celebrate the lives of our children. The "Sanctity of Life" Sunday is also on the calendar at this time. Once every four years, this weekend is normally the time when we celebrate the inauguration of the president. And yes, I think it is significant that the third Monday in January is the national holiday that commemorates the birth and work of Dr. Martin Luther King Jr., who reminded us through his words and leadership that the destiny of all Americans is inextricably woven together. The simple rights that are due all of us as citizens of this country have nothing to do with the color of our skin, our religious background, or our ethnic orientation. Rather, our civil rights have everything to do with the fact that we are citizens of the greatest nation on earth.

How fitting that we explore the second phrase from the Model Prayer, "Your kingdom come, your will be done on earth as it is in heaven." Even to invoke this petition is somehow to get in touch with the very meaning of what the gospel is all about through the life, death, and resurrection of our Lord. Jesus gave his life that you and I might glimpse and experience the kingdom of God in our lives and in our relationships.

When we study the English language we learn that the imperative mood is the mood of command or demand. It may surprise or trouble you that in the Model Prayer there are no less than six imperatives. When you read the prayer in the original language the imperatives literally beat you up because of their profound insistence that God do something in our lives through the experience of prayer. Though they don't sound like imperatives in English, "Hallowed be your name," "your kingdom come," "your will be done," "give us this day," "forgive us our trespasses," and "lead us not" are all imperatives.

The phrase "Your kingdom come, your will be done on earth as it is in heaven" has our attention for a few moments right now. More specifically, this phrase cries out for definition, particularly the definition of the two words "kingdom" and "will." What is the reality Jesus called "the kingdom of God" or, as recorded in the Gospel of Matthew, "the kingdom of heaven"? What does it mean to pray, "your kingdom come"? Obviously, the kingdom of God is the reign of God, the rule of God, the reality of God in our lives and in the world. The kingdom of God is God's reign and rule and reality in every life and in every relationship.

That being so, what an audacious act to pray, "your kingdom come, your will be done on earth as it is in heaven." Will that ever happen? Will any of us or any of our children or any of our grandchildren—will any generation—ever experience the kingdom of God in anything near its fullness? Go to the Bible and you will discover that throughout the writing of the Scriptures in every generation, God's people longed for God's kingdom. The psalms we call the "Enthronement Psalms"—Psalm 93 and Psalms 95–99—all invoke God as king and express a longing for that day when God will be king in every life.

Turn to the prophets and you discover this longing for the coming of the kingdom of God. This prophetic longing is perhaps best found in the prophet Isaiah, who described a day when the wolf would lie down with the lamb and when children would play at the front door of a viper's home (Isa 11:6). According to Isaiah, the kingdom of God would be the moment when all reality would be so transformed that every smidgen of animosity, every vestige of adversity, every experience of conflict would be removed, obliterated from reality, and the kingdom of God would come. What a day that would be!

And then, onto the stage of human and cosmic history strides our Lord, whose first words as he came into Galilee after his baptism and temptation in the desert were these: "The time is fulfilled, the kingdom of God is near; repent, and believe in the good news" (Mark 1:15). If you begin a journey through the Gospels, you will discover that Jesus talked often about the kingdom of God. Let's revisit a few familiar stories. The first is found in John 3, the story about

Jesus' night visitor named Nicodemus. Nicodemus came to Jesus at night because he had heard and seen so much of our Lord's ministry. He was intrigued by what Jesus did and said. Jesus said to Nicodemus, the wise scholar-leader of Israel, "Very truly, I tell you, no one can see the kingdom of God without being born from above' [or born again]" (John 3:3). But what is the kingdom of God? We long to see it, we long to experience it, but how would we ever know if it came?

In Luke 11, we find a little hint. We find a troubling story about Jesus casting out a demon. There, as recorded in Luke 11:20, Jesus said, "But if it is by the finger of God that I cast out the demons, then the kingdom of God has come to you." But what is the kingdom? To attempt an answer, we turn to what may be the most enigmatic passage of all about the kingdom of God found in Luke 17. This is what the record says: "Once Jesus was asked by the Pharisees when the kingdom of God was coming, and he answered, 'The kingdom of God is not coming with things that can be observed; nor will they say, "Look, here it is!" or "There it is!" For the kingdom of God is among you'" (Luke 17:20-21). Another way to translate that last phrase would be, "The kingdom of God is among you," meaning in the Greek, "You all" or "all of you." The question lingers. What is the kingdom of God?

The kingdom of God is the rule and reign of God, the radical reality of God's life as revealed in Jesus in every life and every relationship. The kingdom of God is God's presence and power in our lives and in all lives, indeed in all reality. But how and where and when does that happen? Where do we find the kingdom of God? The next phrase helps us.

Remember, we learned that "Our Father" is interpreted by "Hallowed be your name." Well, "your kingdom come" is most readily interpreted by "your will be done on earth as it is in heaven." Again, the second phrase interprets the first. What does it mean for the kingdom of God to come? It means that God's will is done on earth as it is in heaven. The kingdom of God comes whenever and wherever God's will is done on earth as it is in heaven. How in the world does that happen? What is God's will? And how could God's will come to fuller expression in our lives so we may "see" or experience the kingdom of God?

Before I suggest an answer to that question, let me mention a temptation you and I must face. The temptation is simply this: when we talk about the will of God, the temptation is to "micro-personalize" a definition. The temptation is only to ask, "What is the immediate, small, routine 'will of God' for me?" Meaning, "Should I take this job or that job?" "Is it God's will that I do this or that?" "Is it God's will that I marry this person or that person?" We've all prayed such "will of God" prayers.

I remember hearing of a college student who struggled with which graduate school to attend. So he did a "Gideon" on God. Have you ever "Gideonized" God? Remember the fleece? He put a glass of water in his window. I understand this was a sophisticated person. He put a glass of water in his window and drew a line around the middle of the glass and poured water up to that line. Before he went to bed that night he prayed, "Now God, if you really want me to go to this graduate school, I want the water to be down about a quarter of an inch and then I'll know that is where I'm supposed to go." He got up the next morning and the water level hadn't changed a bit.

So he said, "Maybe that was the wrong prayer." The next night he went to bed and prayed, "Lord, if I'm supposed to go to this other graduate school instead of that one, then let the water go down a quarter of an inch." He went to bed, got up the next morning, and the water level hadn't changed a millimeter.

Let's be honest. When we talk about the will of God, the great temptation in our lives is to micro-personalize it. What am *I* supposed to do? Where am *I* supposed to go? What decisions am *I* supposed to make? Jesus intends something far more significant. Jesus confronts us with "big picture" issues. I suggest that God may not be quite as interested in whether or not you go to this school or that school or buy a Ford or a Chevrolet as in whether or not you are obedient to God with the life God has given you.

Some of you in the next few weeks or months may receive a call from someone asking you to work in a soup kitchen. I don't know who is going to call you; I don't know when the call is coming; but someone may call you with an assignment like that. And you are going to say to that person, "Let me think about that." At that moment, you may be tempted to hang up and go back to fretting about whether or not you need to buy a new car rather than asking God, "What is your will?" According to this prayer and the life and ministry of Jesus, you have it all backwards. The will of God, according to Jesus, is that you and I invest our lives in other people. Whether or not we purchase a new car is far down on the list of priorities, and yet we raise these kinds of things to the top of our consciousness as if they are the important matters of life. "Your kingdom come, your will be done on earth as it is in heaven" has so much to do with our obedience and our faithfulness to God and so little to do with the micro, mini, selfish, self-centered decisions we make day after day.

You say, "Give me some Bible for that." How about Matthew 7:21? "Not everyone who says to me 'Lord, Lord,' will enter the kingdom of heaven, but only the one who does the will of my Father who is in heaven." It really doesn't matter how well you and I sing on Sunday morning in the grand picture of things. It really doesn't matter how eloquently we pray; it really doesn't matter in the big picture whether we use all the right words and get all the theological phrases just right. What does matter is this pesky reality Jesus called "the will of God." Are we *acting* on, behaving in the will of God?

Want another verse? How about five? Matthew 12:46-50.

> While [Jesus] was still speaking to the crowds, his mother and his brothers were standing outside wanting to speak to him. Someone told him, "Look, your mother and your brothers are standing outside, wanting to speak to you." But to the one who had told him this, Jesus replied, "Who is my mother, and who are my brothers?" And pointing to his disciples, he said, "Here are my mother and my brothers! For whoever does the will of my Father in heaven is my brother and sister and mother."

What does that mean? When we pray, "Your kingdom come, your will be done on earth as it is in heaven," we are actually preparing our lives to hear God ask us a life-altering question. What are you going to do about the big picture of the kingdom of God coming in the world? What is your response going to be? How are you going to be faithful? God's kingdom will come to the degree that we are willing to offer ourselves to God in utter and complete obedience to Jesus Christ.

T. W. Manson, the great Anglican scholar, crafted an excellent sentence worth remembering. "There is a sense in which the Kingdom comes whenever and wherever God's will is acknowledged and obeyed on earth."[1] Questions linger: "What does that mean?" "How could I know what the will of God is?" Jesus offers wise and convicting counsel: "You have heard that it was said to those of ancient times, 'You shall not murder'; and 'whoever murders shall be liable to judgment.' But I say to you that if you are angry with a brother or sister, you will be liable to judgment" (Matt 5:21-22). "You are the salt of the earth" (Matt 5:13a), and "You are the light of the world" (Matt 5:14a). "You have heard that it was said, 'You shall not commit adultery.' But I say to you that everyone who looks at a woman with lust has already committed adultery with her in his heart" (Matt 5:27-28).

What is the will of God?

> You have heard that it was said, "An eye for an eye and a tooth for tooth." But I say to you, Do not resist an evildoer. But if anyone strikes you on the right cheek, turn the other also; and if anyone wants to sue you and take your coat, give your cloak as well; and if anyone forces you to go one mile, go also the second mile. Give to everyone who begs from you, and do not refuse anyone who wants to borrow from you. (Matt 5:38-42)

What is the will of God?

> Do not store up for yourselves treasures on earth, where moth and rust consume and where thieves break in and steal. But store up for yourselves treasures in heaven, where neither moth nor rust consume and where thieves do not break in and steal. For where your treasure is, there your heart will be also. (Matt 6:19-20)

What is the will of God? Also read Matthew 6:24-27 and Matthew 7:1-3. Clearly, our Lord taught that God's will is discovered and fulfilled in the daily decisions we make about loyalties, loves, prejudices, money, clothing, and the degree to which we stoop to meet human need. When we make those decisions based upon God's kingdom and God's will, we discover in our own lives the power of Jesus' words. "Everyone then who hears these words of mine and acts on them will be like a wise man who built his house on the rock" (Matt 7:24).

I would suggest to you as I again listen to my own heart of hearts that to pray audaciously and boldly, "Your kingdom come, your will be done, on earth as it is in heaven," is to put all of us in the gravest sort of danger. As best I can read it and as difficult as it is for me to write it, I don't think we honor God or bring glory to the cause of Christ when we ring our hands over our stocks and bonds and worry about our possessions. Sometimes we lose sleep over the hurtful things that have happened to us, most of which were never intended to be malicious. I deeply believe we do not honor God when we spend so much of our time fretting about the things of life that will never endure the passing of time.

"Your kingdom come, your will be done, on earth as it is in heaven." In my judgment, it is God's unmistakable will for every life to know God as love. You may have come to this moment in your life with a lot of religious baggage. You may think being a Christian is all about keeping rules and toeing the mark and checking off a little list of what you think are rights and wrongs. And yet our Lord's life and word clearly teach that unless we are born again we cannot see the kingdom of God. What is the kingdom of God? It begins with a changed heart, a changed life made new by God's unchanging love. What is the kingdom of God? The kingdom of God finds expression in our lives when a changed heart and a changed life gets involved with audacious love in at least one place of need—one little festering sore of human brokenness, one little hurt. Make a difference in that one place by the grace, the power, the love of God. And when you make that difference, at least in that place, the kingdom of God comes.

Prayer

God our Father, glory and praise are rightly and devotedly offered to you as the great King over all our lives and indeed all reality. When we pray "Your Kingdom come," we cannot help longing for your complete rule and reign over our broken and bleeding world.

We especially thank you for the gift of children. We thank you for their unbridled enthusiasm for life, their uncommon acceptance of others, and their willingness to forgive. Remind us today of Jesus' words that all of us must become as children if we are ever to glimpse your Kingdom. Place within all of us a childlike wonder and openness to you and others, that we might see and experience grace in all its power.

God, in whose image we are made and by whose power we are made your children, hear our many prayers. Meet the needs we your children bring to you, not according to our desires, but that your Kingdom may come and your will may be done on earth as it is in heaven. This we pray through Jesus Christ our Lord, whose model prayer continues to be a beacon of strength for all who seek you. Amen.

[1] T. W. Manson, in David Hill, *The Gospel of Matthew*, New Century Bible (Greenwood: The Attic Press, 1978), 137.

Is Daily Bread Enough?

Give us this day our daily bread.
—Matthew 6:11

"Give us this day our daily bread." But is daily bread enough? We have learned that the Lord's Prayer has no less than six imperatives. This prayer demands much from God and summons much from us. These imperatives keep pounding on God's door, hitting God with the demands Jesus taught us to bring to our Father.

When you look at the text in the original language, there is something interesting about the way the prayer is written. Here's a brief language lesson to help us find our place in this prayer of prayers. In the Greek language, the verb normally comes at or near the beginning of the sentence. Once you find and translate the verb, the sentence normally comes together. In this prayer, the imperatives our Lord used normally fall at the beginning of each petition: "Hallowed be thy name," "Your kingdom come, your will be done," "Forgive us our debts," "Lead us not." All those verbs come at the beginning of the phrase. Not so here.

That's why this petition is a bit difficult to unpack. "Give us this day our daily bread," sticks out grammatically, linguistically in the text like a flashing light. The word order is a yellow blinking light saying "Pay attention to me" because it is written differently than the other petitions. The phrase reads literally, "Our daily bread give us today." So this phrase is like the first beginning phrase, "Our Father," in that it begins "Our bread."

Entertain with me three troubling realities in this phrase. Let them trouble you, haunt you, wiggle you around in the land of logic. I have already mentioned the first troubling reality: that the other phrases begin with the imperative. The second troubling reality is that this is the only petition in the prayer where we ask God for something physical for our personal lives. "Give us today our daily bread." It's material, personal, a need we all have. We must never forget that around the world bread is still the staff of life. For billions of people, life is sustained by simple bread. When you travel overseas, one of the things you must do is sample the bread every place you go. People of every nation under heaven know how to bake bread. Jesus taught us to ask God for simple bread.

The third reality in this phrase is the fact, more an observation, that New Testament scholars don't know how to translate it. Pick up any number of translations of the Model Prayer and you will find this phrase translated differently. "Give us today our daily bread." Let's take the words as they come. The first phrase, "Give us." I know it's later in the phrase in the original language, but let me put it first for us English speakers. "Give us." The verb "give" reminds us that as we pray, we remember that God has always been and will always be the eternal, faithful source of everything we need.

The verb "give" summons in the Christian consciousness the reality of "grace." All of us seeking to know God find that this grand discovery is possible not because we are smart, not because we are wise, not because we are good. None of us know God because we are good, placating God with deeds, actions, piety, and what we would call "holy thoughts." Not at all! If we know God at all, we know God because God chose to reveal who God is to us. God sent God's only Son, and through Jesus God offers grace that none of us deserve and can never earn.

Paul was right in that verse we learned in Bible school, "For by grace you have been saved through faith, and this is not your own doing; it is the gift of God" (Eph 2:8). So we are right here to pray "Give," because we know God in Christ as the eternal One whose very nature is to give. That's who God is.

Then we read "Give us." Notice it doesn't say "Give me." It's hard for us contemporaries living at the end of the twentieth century to hear this Bible reality when we are so self-centered. We are not to pray, "Give me today my daily bread," but rather "Give us today our daily bread." This simple petition, like "Our Father," reminds us that we inseparably touch each other and are touched by the weaving hand of God. "Give us."

Here again, the Model Prayer will not let us take our experience of God and privatize it for our own desires, wants, and needs. We cannot be honest with God and shut each other out of our lives. It is not Christian. You can try that, and many live that, but you will live the Christian life unaware of blessed ties that bind your life to others. The Christian life is the life that redeems us individually by the grace of God and puts us in the fellowship of others. We need each other. We can't be Christian without each other. "Give us."

Then the next phrase, "Give us *today*." This word reveals the tricky part of the phrase. One translation renders the phrase, "Give us our bread for today." Eugene Peterson paraphrases it this way in *The Message*: "Keep us alive with three square meals." That is not what I understand Jesus to be teaching us. The people who first learned this prayer in the first century were lucky to have one square meal a day. We are not talking about being well fed with a high calorie, high carbohydrate, low fat, low cholesterol diet. That is not what Jesus taught us to pray. Jesus is teaching us to pray, "Give us today, now, right now what our needs are in this moment, so that we can continue to be faithful to God."

How do you understand that? Let's have Jesus interpret it for us. Look a bit closer at the entire sixth chapter of Matthew. The Model Prayer is found in verses 9-13. In the very center of the prayer is this tricky petition, "Give us this day our daily bread. "Then, in the rest of this chapter, Jesus hammers on the word "today, today, today."

Here are a few examples. Look at verse 19: "Do not store up for yourselves treasures on earth, where moth and rust consume and where thieves break in and steal. "What is our Lord saying? Live the kingdom life today by storing up treasures in heaven. Now let's get more specific. In verses 25-34 he has a word for everybody who lives in the new century: "Do not worry. "Notice specifically what Jesus taught about worry in verse 31 to the end of the chapter. Remember that the operative word is "today."

> Therefore do not worry, saying, "What shall we eat?" or "What shall we drink?" or "What shall we wear?" For it is the Gentiles who strive for all these things; and your heavenly Father knows that you need all these things. But strive first for the kingdom of God and his righteousness, and all these things will be given to you as well. So do not worry about tomorrow, for tomorrow will bring worries of its own. Today's trouble is enough for today.

The prayer's words are "Give us this day." If we could simply learn to trust God one day at a time by living faithfully today and asking God for the privilege of living faithfully tomorrow. So many of us are so anxious about the "what ifs" of life that may never happen, all the while missing today.

When our children were babies, I began praying for them, one specific prayer. I don't think I have ever told them this. I had one big prayer for their lives. It was that they would grow up in the womb of the church and always love God and always love the church. So many ministers' children grow up and they either hate God or they hate the church or they hate both God and the church. As I prayed for them when they were infants, I had to let them go, because there is no way a dad who is also a pastor can control every experience his child would have in the life of a church. I prayed, "Lord, help Kathie and me to be faithful today and place them in churches that will love them. Teach us to trust you with their tomorrows." God has been faithful. God has answered my prayers for their tomorrows and continues to do so one day at a time. "Give us today."

Look at the next phrase. The next words are "daily bread." In his book *Prayer, Finding the Heart's True Home*, Dr. Richard Foster, a Quaker, writes these lines: "The Model Prayer concerns embrace the whole world, from the coming of the Kingdom to daily bread."[1] And it is so true. When we pray this prayer, we discover as we learned from our study of "Our Father" that we must be big-picture Christians. We pray "May your kingdom come" while fully aware that prayer deals with the simple things of life. This petition summons us to bring life's little things to God—life's simple requirements—believing that God is concerned about the daily bread "stuff" of life. You ask, "How is that so?" Look at the life of Jesus. Jesus fed hungry people with ordinary daily bread. Jesus changed ordinary water into wine at an ordinary wedding. Jesus met ordinary people with ordinary needs during ordinary days with God's extraordinary power. "Give us today our daily bread." Daily bread is what you and I need today, trusting that God will provide what we need tomorrow.

What do these verses mean in the life of a church? In my judgment, God meets the ordinary needs of God's people to the degree we are willing to be faithful to God's kingdom. I'm not suggesting that if you and I are faithful to God's church, all of our needs will be met. That's not what I'm saying. But I am saying that in the life of every church you will find some ordinary, basic needs. God looks to adults to care for and nurture children. God calls those of us who are able to manage steps and stairs to be mindful of those in wheelchairs who need ramps. God expects us to return to God tithes and offerings as basic gifts to meet the basic needs of God's church in its local setting and around this needy world.

It has been the custom in the churches I have served as pastor to give Bibles to our first graders. I remember one year in Augusta we had forty-one first graders. In five years, those first graders will move to the youth department. God calls the church to be faithful to its first graders today, knowing well that soon, we will see them tomorrow as teenagers and not long after that as young adults.

Do you see why we must always look toward the future, while always being faithful today? "Give us this day our daily bread." Is daily bread enough? Yes it is.

Because all God calls us to do this moment is to be faithful today and to walk into the vision of tomorrow.

Prayer (Super Bowl Sunday)
Our Father, today is your day. On the first day of the week we celebrate your Son's victorious life over death. For that reason alone, it's Super Sunday. Because He lives, we shall live also. Thank you, Father, for giving us life through Jesus Christ our Lord.

For some this morning, this has been a week of great difficulty. The death of someone dear, the loss of employment, the feared diagnosis, or the unexplainable abandonment are but a few of the hurts some bring to you. We pray today for all who know life's broken places.

Others today are celebrating the birth of a child, the professional promotion, the accomplishment of a friend, or the success of a son or daughter. Theirs is the experience of joy and with them, we who pray rejoice.

If the truth were known, O God, all of us come to this hour with spiritual needs that defy human definition. Our sin has left us empty, our pride has left us lonely, and our many fears have left us immobilized.

Hear our prayers and know our hearts. Confront us with the truth and grant us the courage to act in faith and obedience to your living Word. This we pray through Christ our Lord. Amen.

[1] Richard J. Foster, *Prayer, Finding the Heart's True Home* (San Francisco: HarperSanFrancisco, 1992), 184.

Conditional, Unqualified Forgiveness

And forgive us our debts, as we also have forgiven our debtors.
—Matthew 6:9-13

Forgive, and you will be forgiven.
—Luke 6:37

The title of this chapter puts us in great difficulty. The difficulty posed does not lie in a title like "Conditional, Unqualified Forgiveness," but rather in the twelfth verse of Matthew 6. That line says, "Forgive us our debts as we also have forgiven our debtors." The key word is *as*. Another way of translating this verse from the original language is 'Free us from what we owe you, God, even as we have already freed those who owe us."

This poses great difficulty for us packaged in liberation language. Whether you render the word as "debts," or whether you render it "trespasses" as in the Model Prayer from the Book of Common Prayer, the idea is the same: we are to ask God to release us from all the spiritual liens upon our lives to the degree that we have already let go of the liens we have on others. "Forgive us our debts as we have already forgiven our debtors."

This sounds like the Golden Rule: "Do to others as you would have them do to you" (Matt 7:12). The question bubbling in my mind and perhaps in yours is simply this: Is Jesus saying that we have no right to ask God for forgiveness for sins we commit against God unless we have forgiven those who have sinned against us? We fear that is exactly what he is saying.

If this troubles you, take comfort. The disciples were troubled by it as well. Look at the verses that follow the Model Prayer in Matthew 6. There, we discover that Jesus interpreted this troubling line from the prayer (Matt 6:14-15). In fact, these are the only lines from the Model Prayer our Lord interpreted in the Sermon on the Mount. "For if you forgive others their trespasses, your heavenly Father will also forgive you; but if you do not forgive others, neither will your Father forgive your trespasses." I don't know how Jesus could have put it any clearer. Lest we think this is some isolated teaching of Jesus or think perhaps this is not actually what Jesus meant, look closer. Look back one chapter to Matthew 5:21-24: "You have heard that it was said to those of ancient times, 'You shall not murder'; and 'whoever murders will be liable to judgment.' But I say to you that if you are angry with a brother or sister you will be liable to judgment." Keep reading. "So when you are offering your gift at the altar, if you remember that your brother or sister has something against you, leave your gift there before the altar and go; first be reconciled to your brother or sister and then come and offer your gift."

Did Jesus say you can kill someone without killing them? Yes, he did. Then he said that if you and I are doing our outward acts of piety in public and remember that a brother or a sister has something against us, some debt, something that is owed us in terms of relationship, we had better leave our gift before the altar and go and first be reconciled to our brother or sister. Only then can we come back and continue our worship. Is that truly what Jesus meant? Think not that these are isolated sayings of our Lord.

Go to Matthew 18. In verses 21-35 we have one of our Lord's more lengthy parables. Jesus told the parable of the unmerciful servant after Peter asked how many times should he forgive his brother. Seven times? Jesus said, "No, not seven times, but seventy times seven." Then Jesus told the parable about a person who was forgiven a great debt, who then, forgiven of the debt, found someone who owed him a pittance. He grabbed him by the throat and wouldn't let him go until he paid his debt. Jesus pronounced stern judgment on such arrogance. Notice the last verse of the parable: "So my heavenly Father will also do to every one of you, if you do not forgive your brother or sister from your heart" (v. 35).

We must rethink forgiveness. Jesus is saying that hatred, bigotry, belligerence, sarcasm, innuendo, gossip, hostility, meanness, or what we call "old-fashioned cussedness" is out of place in the kingdom of God. Forgive us, liberate us, free us from our sins against you, O God, to the degree that we practice forgiveness toward others.

Someone is thinking right now, *I simply don't believe that. I don't have to forgive what he did.* Or *You don't know what she did to me.* Or *You don't know what he said about me.* Matthew 6:14-15 (NIV) says, "For if you forgive others when they sin against you, your Heavenly Father will also forgive you. But if you do not forgive men their sins your Father will not forgive you.*"* What do we do with this?

These verses leave us troubled and put us in no small degree of danger. What is Jesus saying? The fact that we are so troubled by our Lord's teaching on forgiveness tells me this is clear-varnish gospel. It troubles us so much that it must be the word of God. Unqualified forgiveness from God requires unqualified forgiveness of others. If you and I want to live in a free, open, and forgiving relationship with God, we have no right or basis to seek God's pardon if we are not ready, willing, active, and intentional about living a life of reconciliation with other people.

There's more in the Bible. Look at Luke 11:2-4. There you will find Luke's version of the Model Prayer. In Luke 11, the troubling line is rendered with even greater boldness: "And forgive us our sins, for we ourselves forgive everyone indebted to us." Unqualified forgiveness from God requires unqualified, generous forgiveness of others.

This petition tells us something else: Forgiveness *is* conditional, not forgiveness *may be* conditional. Forgiveness *is* conditional. Look in Luke 6:37. This is a text from the Sermon on the Plain. It's Dr. Luke's account of this same teaching from the Sermon on the Mount, the sermon from which the Model Prayer comes. "Do not judge, and you will not be judged; do not condemn, and you will not be condemned. Forgive, and you will be forgiven." It seems that forgiveness is conditional.

Am I saying God's forgiveness is contingent upon our forgiveness? No. I'm simply reporting to you what Jesus said. Why is that so? Why does forgiveness work that way? Two words: the first word is *accountability*. There is no such thing as a Christian life that is not accountable to God and to others. Christianity is not a live-anyway-you-please, do-whatever-you-feel, treat-people-anyway-you-want faith. There is an accountability woven into the gospel.

Gospel accountability also calls us to be people of *responsibility*. In the business of doing life, we are broken, sinful, errant, duplicitous, wishy-washy, mean, human beings. Though we have been freed by the grace of God from the penalty and the sentence of sin and hell, we are still subject to the reality of sin. As we live in relationship with other people, we discover to our pain and even shame that all relationships have broken sides.

I'm aware that what I'm saying is difficult to hear. It could simply be a preacher problem in your mind, and indeed there is a sense in which this is a problem for the preacher. From my point of view, living in this skin, I have no idea of the pain or the hurt or the history or the difficulty through which you are living. When the mere thought of forgiving "so-and-so" crosses your mind, you find yourself in an angry, painful place. "You mean I have to forgive him?" "What makes you so self-righteous, so sanctimonious, so pompous to tell me what I have to do?" I'm aware of the preacher problem.

But I am also aware that with the reality of sin and brokenness in our lives, there is also the greater reality of grace. We often live with such hostility and animosity, revenge and get-evenness, that we harbor things against a brother or sister that are one, two, ten, twenty, thirty, or more years old. When we do, we create a grace deficit in our souls. This grace deficiency is so deadly, so damaging, and so wounding that God's grace stops flowing through our lives. This happens not because God's grace is insufficient. Not at all. It happens because our attitudes short-circuit the grace of God.

Let me be practical. You may be saying, "Let me think about how I can do this. How can I bring about reconciliation from the person or people with whom I am at odds?" Let me offer some thoughts.

My first suggestion would be to write the person a letter. In that letter, tell him or her three things. First, tell about your pain: "I'm hurting. I'm broken. You wounded me with your words, you embarrassed me, and you brought sorrow on my family. To say it didn't hurt would be a lie. It hurt then and still hurts." Next, release that person from your hurt. Forgive them. Remember that Jesus said, "Forgive and you will be forgiven." Say "I forgive you" and let it go. Here's the tough one. In that same letter, ask the person to forgive you. More importantly, ask them to forgive you for carrying around in your soul the destructive emotions of revenge, bitterness, malice, and even bodily harm or worse. If you do these things, you communicate a powerful reality. Write the letter. It might open the door for a new relationship.

Perhaps writing letters isn't your forte. Instead, do something wonderful for that person and do it anonymously. Send flowers. Do something thoughtful or kind.

If the person has died, moved away, or if you're unable to write a letter or do something kind for them, try imagining a visit with them. In that visit, let the hurt go. Have the person sit in your living room, or imagine going to their living room. Have a mental conversation and tell them you let them go. In that imaginary conversation, ask them to let you go. Forgive and you will be forgiven. "Forgive us what we owe you, even as we have already forgiven those who owe us."

I have experienced one of those touching moments of pastoral ministry that a minister never forgets. It's a tender memory of an encounter that happened many years ago, but it's as if it occurred yesterday. He came to see me. He was a long-time member of our church. In his seventies, he was an avid reader, a faithful and loving churchman. I preached a sermon on forgiveness. A few days later, he came to see me. "Preacher, is what you said Sunday true? That God's forgiveness is all wrapped up in our ability to forgive others?" I said, "As best I understand the gospel, that's what it says." He said, "I've got a problem." "What is it?" "I was a bombardier in World War II and flew many missions over Germany. I can still see through that scope those bombs falling on Dresden and Cologne and Berlin. Can God forgive me?" He went on. "I can't ask those people. I don't know how to ask all those people to forgive me."

I said to him, "Let's bring them all into the study." In the next few moments, I witnessed in my study the transformation of a human being by the power of God. For the first time in forty years, he felt the guilt and shame, the pain and horror of those war years roll out of his soul.

If you say to God today, not to me, that you can't or won't forgive someone, tell God that. No. Tell God you will. Because if you and I will let go of the hurts in our lives that others, either with intentionality and malice or through ignorance and omission, have inflicted upon us, we will find forgiveness and grace and the love of God unlike any we have known in our lives.

Prayer
Our Father, you hold us with love that has borne the terror of crucifixion and the sorrow of abandonment. In your Son, Jesus Christ, you stooped to the depths of bitter tragedy, experiencing the hell of death that we might be brought on wings of life into your presence.

We who claim your grace cling to no merit of our own. If we were all honest today, we would confess that sin has shaken us to the depths of our being and left us for dead. We are—all of us—lost and in need of a Savior.

As we journey through the season of Lent, turn our self-centered lives again to hear the voice of Jesus. Cause us to heed the invitation to take up the cross and follow him. And yes, may the lessons he taught of sacrifice and surrender engrave their promise into all our lives.

God of limitless love and freeing forgiveness, lest we ever think we have it all together, dismember every idol we have made and so trouble us by your Spirit that we will not rest until we lay all we are and all we have and all we dream before your nail-pierced feet, for you alone are worthy.

Hear every heart and summon every life through Jesus Christ, to whom be glory and praise and worship now and always. Amen.

Deliverance from Evil's Temptation

And do not bring us to the time of trial,
but rescue us from the evil one.
—Matthew 6:13

I'm haunted by the last phrase of the Model Prayer: "And do not bring us to the time of trial, but rescue us from the evil one." You may have a footnote in your Bible that says, "Deliver us *from evil*," as you and I are used to praying when we pray the Lord's Prayer. The text seems to indicate that the best way to translate the phrase is that we ask God to deliver us from the "evil one" or the "evil being." And of course the one who comes to mind is the person of Satan, or the devil. You will remember earlier in the Gospel of Matthew that Jesus faced temptation with the devil in the desert. So it is not out of character for this petition to end the prayer. Jesus is teaching us that we too need to ask God to deliver us from the "evil one."

Perhaps a more literal translation of this phrase would read something like this: "And *never* lead us to the test." *Never.* In the Greek language, there is a strong negative (*me*) that is more accurately brought into English as *No* or *Never.* Anytime you see the Greek word *me*, it indicates a strong negative. Here, Jesus is saying, "God, never lead us to the test." Though the New Revised Standard Version translates the word "trial," I know we are used to the word "temptation." We are going to take a close look at that below. For now, a better translation is "never lead us to the trial" or "to the test for our faith," "but rather rescue us from the evil one. "We ask God not to bring us to the test, but rather to bring us away from the evil one.

Let's look at this first phrase in first century context. It is difficult for us today in the relative post-9/11 safety of America to think about being persecuted for our Christian faith. As I was surfing *The New York Times* on the Internet a few years ago, I pulled from the February 11, 1997, issue an op-ed piece titled "Persecuting the Christians." It was written by a Jew. The writer's name was Rosenthal. He wrote about the problem of Christians under persecution. He then noted that at that time, there were eleven countries in the world, many with which we have diplomatic relations, whose governments were either persecuting Christians or looking the other way while Christians suffered persecution for their faith—China, Saudi Arabia, and the Sudan, in which he noted there was an outright pogrom taking place in which Christian villages were burned, children killed, and priests executed. We don't like to think about that. Most Christians in the non-western world have no choice: they pray the Model Prayer differently than we do because they live in the gaping jaws of threatened persecution.

Jesus is teaching us that when we pray, we must pray as men and women who are aware of the environment in which we live. Make no mistake about it. Jesus had a simple message, but he was not naive. He knew that it was costly and would be costly to follow him. Let's follow this idea of trial and testing through the New Testament. First, let's look at trials for believers as revealed in the Gospel of Matthew and elsewhere in the New Testament. In Matthew 10, we find what could be called the great discipleship chapter of the gospel in which Jesus, in the first part of the chapter, sends out the twelve on a missionary journey. Our Lord instructs them to go out and preach and then come back later and give him a report of their mission.

Notice carefully in Matthew 10 that after Jesus instructs the disciples in the first sixteen verses, in verse 17 he begins to talk more about the trials of being a Christian believer. "Beware of them." This command doesn't mean we are to be against others; it means we are to be on our guard. We are to be "aware" Christians. Remember that Jesus had a simple message, but he wasn't naive. "Beware of them, for they will hand you over to councils and flog you in their synagogues." Who was the best-known apostle to whom this happened? Paul. Paul preached the gospel in cities by first going to the synagogue. What happened there? They threw him out. Jesus saw such a moment as recorded in Matthew 10:18-20:

> And you will be dragged before governors and kings because of me, as a testimony to them and the Gentiles. When they hand you over, do not worry about

how you are to speak or what you are to say; for what you are to say will be given to you at that time; for it is not you who speak, but the Spirit of your Father speaking through you.

Jesus then told the disciples how difficult life would become: "Brother will betray brother to death, and a father his child, and children will rise against parents and have them put to death,; and you will be hated by all because of my name" (Matt 10:21-22a). Jesus is saying to them and to us that trials will come because we follow him.

Look now at verses 26-28:

So have no fear of them; for nothing is covered up that will not be uncovered, and nothing secret that will not become known. What I say to you in the dark, tell in the light; and what your heart whispered, proclaim from the housetops. Do not fear those who kill the body but cannot kill the soul; rather fear him who can destroy both soul and body in hell.

Jesus pulled no punches as he continued in verses 34-36:

Do not think that I have come to bring peace to the earth; I have not come to bring peace, but a sword. For I have come to set a man against his father, and a daughter against her mother, and a daughter-in-law against her mother-in-law; and one's foes will be members of one's own household.

This is the kind of testing that would come to the first Christians and is still coming to some of our brothers and sisters in the world for being Christian and practicing the Christian faith.

"Do not put us to the test." The recited version we know so well prays, "Lead us not into temptation." When we read or recite this phrase, we tend to think about some temptation to commit an immoral act. But that is not what Jesus is teaching here. The word our Lord uses in the Model Prayer is the Greek word *pierosmos.* The other Greek word we associate with temptation to immoral behavior is the word *skandalon*, from which we get the English word "scandal." What Jesus is talking about here are the trials, the tests that come because you are a Christian. These are the temptations that come, inviting us to flee being true to our faith. And what would some of those trials look like in these early years of the twenty-first century?

For one, we are tempted to treat others of different skin color or ethnic origin with contempt. For another, we can speak in ways that disparage the opposite sex, or worse, treat the opposite sex in ways that diminish their humanity. Church leaders are tempted to renounce the role of servant and hold on to power rather than live a life of humility and generosity before others. Christians who are registered to vote are tempted to vote their pocketbook rather than their conscience. The list of trials that come to Christians in our society is long.

When we stand for Christian principles and we refuse to bow to the trials that come our way, what happens? We know. We are often subject to ridicule, to disenfranchisement from others, to abandonment from friends, to betrayal all because the principles taught by our Lord are more important than some temporary benefit. This is, in my judgment, what Jesus is talking about.

Let's look at two other places in the New Testament where this is illustrated. James 1:2 captures our Lord's teaching and applies it to a congregation of early Christians in Jerusalem: "My brothers and sisters, whenever you face trials of any kind, consider it nothing but joy, because you know that the testing of your faith produces endurance; and let endurance have its full effect, so that you may be mature and complete, lacking in nothing." Here, James is writing to people who are under persecution. If I may paraphrase, he says, "Celebrate when you are tried. If you are going to have a trial, throw a party." "Whenever you face trials of any kind, consider it nothing but joy." Why? Because the testing of your faith verifies that your faith is true, that you are being true to Christ.

Look at 1 Peter 4:12. "Beloved, do not be surprised at the fiery ordeal that is taking place among you to test you, as though something strange were happening to you." What's Peter saying? When trials come for being a Christian, don't say, "Why is that happening? Why are these people not being kind to me because I am a Christian?" Mistreatment, ridicule, and scorn shouldn't surprise anyone following Jesus. In fact, the negative reaction from others is normal. That is the way the world relates to people who are Christian. Don't let it bother you.

The truth of the matter is, it bothers us, doesn't it? I'm thinking about my young friends—teenagers and young adults—and I know it is tough at school. When peer pressure is heavy and they say, "Hey, there's 'holy Joe' carrying a Bible" or "There's some Christian," the feelings are brutal. Truth to tell, it doesn't get any easier for the rest of us. The stakes just get higher.

It doesn't get any easier for men and women who are in the public eye day after day, whether they be before the bar of justice or in the world of business or in the classroom or in the hospital or wherever. It doesn't get any easier to stand for the principles you believe to be right. When we stand for Christ, we should never wonder why there is opposition from certain quarters. We should expect it. That's what Peter says. If it comes, don't let it bother you. In fact, it's going to come. Don't let it bother you. Persecution is normal. That's what Jesus meant in the Model Prayer: "Lead us not to the test or trial."

Now let's look at that other word in the New Testament for "temptation." The word *scandalon*, from which we get the word scandal, is often translated "stumbling block." It means a temptation that comes to us to lapse or fail morally: some moral temptation such as the temptation to disobey the Ten Commandments, to break God's moral Law. You find the word *scandalon* twenty-two times in the New Testament, three of which are in the Gospel of Matthew. In Matthew 13:40, amid the parable of the tares and the weeds, Jesus says, "Just as the weeds are collected and burned up with fire, so will it be at the end of the age. The Son of Man will send his angels, and they will collect out of his kingdom all causes of sin and all evildoers." The word translated "all causes of sin" is *scandalon*: those things that cause moral failure.

This same word is found in Matthew 16:22-23, where we read of our Lord's first passion prediction and Peter's response. "Peter took him aside and began to rebuke him, saying, 'God forbid it, Lord! This must never happen to you.' But [Jesus] turned and said to Peter, 'Get behind me, Satan! You are a stumbling block to me; for you are setting your mind not on divine things but on human things.'" What does this word often translated "temptation" mean? It means anything that comes into our lives that causes us to be tempted to do or act in ways contrary to the life and teaching of Jesus.

Paul used this word in Romans 16:17: "I urge you, brothers and sisters, to keep an eye on those who cause dissensions and offenses, in opposition to the teaching that you have learned; avoid them." Paul uses *scandalon* to tell the people to be weary of those who want to lead them to do what is contrary to the teaching of Jesus.

These texts and many more tell us that trials for believers are going to come. They often come in ways that tempt us to renounce our faith. They come at times and in ways that would lead us to break God's moral law.

The second thing I want you to see in this verse, "And lead us not to the test, but deliver us from the evil one," is the reality of the "evil one." I'm sure there are differing opinions about the being or reality of Satan. That's okay. But the New Testament has a way of framing life in simple terms. The New Testament puts a frame around reality that says, "All reality is framed in a cosmic battle between God and the forces that are contrary to God." I wish it were not so. I wish I could tell you that evil is a figment of our imagination. I wish I could say, "You don't need to worry about the evil one; that's something they invented in the first century. We are sophisticated today and we don't need to worry about that."

All of us, whether we lived through the second World War and the Holocaust, or whether we have lived in recent years through the madness of the killing fields of Cambodia or the ethnic cleansing in the Balkans, cannot afford to be naive anymore. "Deliver us from the evil one."

The Bible reminds us that you and I live in a world where we have multiple choices and one large choice. We face this large choice every day of our lives. We face it at almost every turn of life. When presented with the choice of being obedient to God in Christ or being disobedient, we have the choice of honoring God with our lives or dishonoring God with our lives. There are times when we choose to honor God with our lives and, when we do, we discover the wonder, the blessing, and the joy of following Christ. Sadly, there are times when we choose to dishonor God with our lives. When we do, we discover the guilt and the shame, the pain and the hurt that come with making that choice. Paul rightly observed, "The wages of sin is death" (Rom 6:23). The Scriptures remind us that the evil one is a reality in our world. We must not be naive.

Let's get back to the Model Prayer. "Never lead us to the test, but rather deliver us from the jaws of the evil one." Let me apply that in two ways. First, God does not lead us to the place of testing. I know again there will be differences of opinions about my interpretation. Would that we could have dialogical relationship beyond the pages of this book! I know I can go to the Bible with you and I can take you to stories in the Bible where it clearly states that God tested people. For example, God tested Abraham to see if Abraham would be obedient to God.

But I have an understanding of the revelation in the Bible that some of you may share, and that is that God was always revealing more of who God is until God revealed God's perfect revelation in Jesus Christ. If Abraham's understanding of God was sufficient, Jesus would have never had to come as the incarnate Son. I understand the Bible to reveal not only the person of God, but also an unfolding in human consciousness of who God is until we get to Jesus, about whom the writer of Hebrews says, "He is the full revelation of God" (Heb 1:1). If you want to know who God is, look at Jesus. He is the perfect, fulfilled revelation of God.

Jesus teaches us in this prayer that we are to say to God, "Never lead us to the test." That doesn't mean we will not be tested. We have already seen from the Gospel of Matthew, from James, from Peter, and from other evidence in the New Testament that Christians will be tested. Testing for being a Christian is going to happen.

So what is unique here? What these and other stories suggest is that rather than God leading us to the test, God meets us in the test. See the difference? God says (as I paraphrase several passages from the New Testament), "My strength is sufficient for you. I will be there with you when you go before the governors and the kings and the rulers. My Spirit will speak through you." How? "I will be there with you." God does not lead us to the place of the test, but the Bible clearly teaches God is with us in the test.

Let's look at a passage of Scripture that helps us understand that: First Corinthians 10:13. My pastor in my teenage years told me to underline and star this verse and I did. I have always gone back to it because it has been a source of strength to me. "No testing has overtaken you that is not common to everyone. God is faithful, and he will not let you be tested beyond your strength, but with the testing he will also provide the way out so that you may be able to endure it." God does not lead us to the place of trial, but God is with us in the trial. Paul is saying to the Corinthians, "God is opening a door there amid the trial for you to be faithful."

Flip Wilson, whom no one less than twenty knows, was wrong. The devil has never made a one of us do anything. Don't ever cop out on God or yourself and say, "Well, you just don't understand. The devil made me do it." Baloney! The devil never makes us do anything. He tempts us. According to James, our own lusts tempt us, but with every temptation there is a way of escape.

Jesus put it this way, "O God, never lead us to the test for our faith, but rather at every point where we are tempted to disobey you and be devoured by the evil one." Rescue us. Give us enough gumption to look around us and see that there is a way out of this. It may take courage, and it may take guts, and it may take ridicule, but it will lead to life. Jesus was last remembered by the writer of the Gospel of Matthew as saying to his disciples these wonderful words: "Go therefore and make disciples of all nations, baptizing them in the name of the Father and of the Son and of the Holy Spirit, and teaching them to obey everything that I have commanded you. And remember, I am with you always, to the end of the age."

The Model Prayer begins with "Our Father." It ends with a prayer for deliverance from the death-dealing ways of the evil one. As you pray this prayer into the future that God has for you, I pray for you as I pray for myself that it will be our chart and compass and strength; that we will weave it deeply into the fabric of our lives.

Prayer
God of mercy, grace, and love, we who are formed in your image often cower in fear before the difficulties of life. We confess that we trust you too little while entrusting ourselves to life's terrors too much. Forgive us, we pray. Forgive us for our lapse of memory, for failing to call to mind the many times in our lives when you soothed our troubled hearts, mended our torn histories, and reconfigured

our fragile egos. You have always been there, will always be there, almighty and loving God.

Open our eyes to see the abundance of your grace. Like a field of dancing flowers, your love has brought spring to the winter of life. When all appeared to be lost, you found us and brought us home. Now, in the strength of your many gifts, we ask for the courage to live faithfully for you when life gets difficult. When another's anger would incite us to hate, awaken within us your love. When the injustices of our time would lead us to give up and walk away from those in need, call us again to give to others as you have so richly given to us.

God of tender mercy and renewing hope, deliver us from the snare of self-righteous security, so that we may joyfully and confidently worship you with our whole lives by giving ourselves to others in love. Through Jesus Christ, your Son and our Savior, we pray. Amen.

Ears that Hear

Sit for Supper

Make them sit down. —Luke 9:14

Jesus has called the twelve together and sent them out on a preaching mission. We are told they went out and preached, healed, and shared the good news with many. The twelve now return to Jesus, no doubt wearied by their travels and exhausted from their work. Being the Good Shepherd, Jesus takes his men aside for a brief retreat. But the crowds pursue them. There is little rest for the weary, and at the end of the day, the twelve come to Jesus not knowing how to meet the hunger of the people. Jesus has the twelve instruct the crowd to "sit down in groups of about fifty." Here, in what the disciples call "a deserted place," Jesus feeds the 5,000 with five loaves and two fish. Weary disciples and hungry people all sit down for supper.

Physician Richard Swenson has written a provocative book with the simple title *Margin*. It's an incredible book. He says in the foreword that it took him ten years to write the book. Dr. Swenson gathers from his clinical experience incredible wisdom about the way we human beings do life. In all of our lives, he writes, we need margin, what he calls white space. We need breathing room—elbow room. What is margin?

Margin is knowing that you have an appointment downtown that requires a fifteen-minute drive. In planning your day, you say to yourself, "I'm going to allow twenty-five minutes to get there just in case I meet an accident, a train, or a funeral procession. Or in case I catch every light on my route. I'm going to create a bit of margin. And if I get there early, I'm going to tell them I'm there, sit down and leaf through a magazine, catch my breath, maybe even pick up the Gideon Bible in the lobby. I'm going to take some time for me." Swenson calls this time "margin." On the other hand, not having any margin "is not having time to finish that book you're reading on stress; margin is having the time to read it twice."[1] He makes a telling observation. As our society has enjoyed greater progress, we have suffered from less margin. Look at the world. The countries with the greatest progress have the largest populations with the least margin. What's going on here?

Let me give you another bit of data Swenson compiled that might help you understand this better. He notes that life generally has five dimensions: the physical, the cognitive, the social, the emotional, and the spiritual. Progress is taking place in the first two, the physical world (more technology) and the cognitive world (more information). But in the social, emotional, and spiritual arenas, we are headed in the other direction. Higher crime, higher incidence of compromised mental health, higher divorce rates, higher difficulties in rearing children, lack of time to pray, meditate, read the Bible, worship.[2]

Are we listening to Dr. Swenson, who thumps on people every day in his office, who orders lab work on his patients and listens to them while observing their lifestyles? Are we listening to ourselves? More progress, less margin.

Sit for supper. Most of us sit for hours at a time at our jobs, in our homes, even during leisure activities (think about a golf cart!). And yes, we sit for much of a worship service in church. We have our bottoms on the pew. I wonder, though, what is the orientation of our souls? We are in a church sanctuary, but where are our minds? We are "there" physically, but where are we?

For years, my mom did something unique when her children came to see her. She would do this whether we sat for breakfast, lunch, or dinner. When company was at her house, particularly her children, when one of us or all of us had our knees under her table, my mother had difficulty sitting for the meal. Did you have a mom like that? One Saturday evening when mom and dad were visiting us, I told her I was going to tell on her in the sermon the next morning. Puzzled, she asked, "Is it a bad story?" I said, "No, Mom. It's simply you." Can you see her? Moving around her kitchen to attend to every one of our needs.

You may have a memory of your mother eating with her apron on, bounding between the table and the kitchen as if she was tied to a stretched rubber band. Every once in a while, when I'm at Mom's house, I say, "Mom, please just sit down." And she does.

I wonder about you. I wonder in this moment if you could savor enough of God's grace to sit for supper. The twelve disciples had gone out on a heavy mission. Think about it. Luke says the disciples "went through the villages, bringing the good news and curing diseases everywhere" (Luke 9:6). That's the stuff Jesus did. This was demanding, draining work. There they were, out doing the same things Jesus was doing. Then they returned home, back to their teacher. I wonder in that moment if their lives were bubbling with joy or if they were exhausted from their work. Jesus gives us the answer. He looked into their eyes and said to himself, "They may be satisfied with their success, but they are worn out." So he said to them, "Come away."

Notice in the text that they are not alone for long. The crowd soon follows (Luke 9:11). The crowds are there, always there—pursuing, hounding, wanting more of Jesus. Like sharks in a feeding frenzy, they want more Jesus. Luke tells us it was late in the afternoon. The day was spent, memories made, time expended, another day slipping away with the sun slithering beneath the western sky. The disciples looked out and saw the crowd. Their reaction, tired now, was "Get rid of them. Send them away." Jesus looked at them and said, "You guys feed them." This is one of the more comic moments in the New Testament. Please read the Bible with a sense of humor. Unbutton your collar, put on an old pair of jeans, loosen up, cozy up to the text. "Send them away." "No, you feed them," said Jesus. "Right, Jesus. No problem. Except all we've got are five loaves and two fish." Our resources, our solutions, our ideas all put together add up to a fish snack. It's what we have and it's not much.

Now notice what Jesus did. He said to the disciples, "Make them sit down." And Luke tells us that they all sat down in groups of fifty: fifty here, fifty there, fifty on that side of the hill, fifty at the bottom of the hill. We are talking 5,000 men, not counting the women and children present. Imagine 150 to 200 groups. Five loaves and two fish. Then we are told that as they were made to sit down, Jesus took those gifts, multiplied them, and everyone was fed.

Imagine that you are seated before a table with bread and wine. To sit there is to be seated before a table with ominous memory. We are seated, but what about our souls? What about our spirits? What about our beings? There is more than food and drink on that table. In that space, before that table may be dozens of blistered souls weary of shuffling here and there, from juggling all the things we think are important. All the things that crowd our lives are there and yet we sit, in this moment, with these simple things, so that God might say to us with alarming clarity what is most important. Sit down.

Our problem today, however, is more troubling. Even though we are seated, we are not often resting. How is it in your soul? I will sit down in my wonderful, overstuffed chair, my body in the chair, but I'm not all there. I'm thinking about that committee or that crisis, or the next sermon or the person in my life who has a special need. Like you, I'm thinking about a dozen other things. My body is in the chair but my mind is in a dozen other places.

Perhaps you stretch out on that sofa and click on the football game. Or you pick up a book, and the game rolls on, or you leaf through the pages of a book as you try to get into the game or vainly attempt to go where the author of the book wants to take you. But all your half-baked efforts are of no use.

Did you hear Jesus? Sit down.

You say, "I don't have anything." Of course you don't. None of us have anything. We are hungry, empty-handed, dry-mouthed beggars. That's why the gospel keeps coming back to us speaking of grace and spiritual food and telling us what God offers. We don't have the resources to feed ourselves. In fact, left to ourselves—more progress, less margin—we know what we do. We exhaust our bodies and our spirits, limp to the doctor and ask her why we are sick. We are sick, no doubt, for many reasons, one of the biggest being that we don't sit for supper. We don't sit physically. We don't sit relationally. We are at all points on the compass except at the seated point.

Did you notice what the text says about people sitting down? Did you notice the inclusive word "all"? They "all" sat down (Luke 9:15). There's a wonderful truth in this text that we need to hang on our lives. If we will sit down, someone might come and sit down with us. But we are not so inclined. We keep moving around like billiard balls on a table. Truth be told, we may stay in frenetic motion because we are frightened that someone may sit down with us, may actually touch us, may come too near our wounded souls.

Can you imagine what would have happened if a couple of people like us had been on the hillside that afternoon? "Make them all sit down." "I'm not going to do it. I'm going to stand up so I can see what is going on here." If you would sit down, Dad, your daughter or your son might sit down with you and you might really get to know them. Mom, if you would just sit down, your husband might sit down with you. Husbands, if you would sit down, you might discover that you really did marry that woman for all the right reasons. Sit down.

It was sometime after this moment that Jesus gathered these guys into an upper room. We are told that on that night of nights in the upper room, they were all seated. In the first century manner, they actually reclined around tables. In that moment, our Lord took bread and cup, food and drink, and said to them, "You know, guys, I don't know if you have ever gotten it, but I'm going to tell it straight one more time tonight. What really feeds you, what can nourish and sustain your life, are not the loaves and the fish. Nor is it the "all-you-can-eat" bar served at the world's buffet. What can truly sustain your life, if you will sit down long enough, is the food of sacrifice, the drink of outpoured love; this is what will sustain you."

Here you are before a table with bread and wine; another Sunday, another church service, another communion. Excuse me for being frank, but the bread is probably stale and the drink is not rare vintage. I can't help but wonder if when these gifts are placed in your hands, your empty hands, your needy hands, if you will let the food and drink of God tell you, "You can sit down." If you will sit down, God will feed you. Some of you don't believe me. Some of you have lived decades and you have never sat down long enough to let God do what God says God will do for you.

Stop being so busy. Stop trying to figure it all out. Rest in amazing grace and great love. Sit down and watch what God does with the simple things that are before you.

[1] Richard A. Swenson, *Margin: Restoring Emotional, Physical, Financial, and Time Reserves to Overloaded Lives* (Colorado Springs: Navpress, 1992), 13.

[2] Ibid., 36-37.

Earthlinks with God

Forgive, and you will be forgiven. — Luke 6:37

Let me give voice to one of the gnawing questions of our humanity: How can I find spiritual satisfaction in a busy, crowded, demanding life? We prize satisfaction at so many levels of our existence. We live in a culture, particularly in the business climate, where anything less than a satisfying experience is unacceptable. When you purchase an automobile or go to the department store and purchase clothing, or if you frequent a certain restaurant, before long all kinds of overtures are made to you asking why you bought that car, are you satisfied with the service, is the product working correctly for you.

Gnawing in the depths of our being is this ultimate question: How can I find spiritual satisfaction? Over the years, I have asked people to complete sermon questionnaires, telling me issues they would like addressed in my preaching. At times, I have asked people to write a question they had that I was not answering from the pulpit. With several surveys I noticed a common question. Let me give you three expressions of it: "How do I link up with God?" "How can I deepen my spiritual life?" "How can I experience forgiveness deeply in my being?" These people didn't need the surface remark, "I'm sorry, you are forgiven. It's okay." Instead, they wanted to plumb the depths of forgiveness and experience deeply spiritual forgiveness.

All of these questions are related to each other. Jesus talked about them candidly in so many places in his teaching. But I don't think he addressed the issue any more clearly than in chapter 6 of the Gospel of Luke. Jesus explodes our understandings about God-link, about deep spiritual satisfaction, and about experiencing forgiveness. If we were presented these questions, we would be tempted to give an ethereal, spiritual, numinous, "holy" answer. How do I link up with God? How do I know spiritual satisfaction? How do I experience forgiveness? We would say, "You've got to pray more." Or, we might ask, "Are you going to church?"

I am absolutely convinced that there are individuals who sit in churches every week who are not hooking up with God. They are not linking with God. They attend a church Sunday after Sunday, sing the songs, hear the Scriptures, sit through the sermon, go out to their car and say, "Well, I've checked that off this week." But checking off the service as if it were the same as going to the grocery store does not address one's deep spiritual emptiness. If praying, attending church, singing hymns, and hearing sermons would link us up with God, we would all have been there a long time ago.

It is interesting how Jesus answers our questions. Jesus turns them around 180 degrees. Jesus says the place we begin is not up in the ethereal air of piety. Rather, he suggests that if we want to link up with God, the place we begin is in the earthy realities of life. We begin with the grime and the dirt, the mess and the reality of human existence. Jesus gives us in this text what I call three earthlinks that can connect us with God.

The first is a refusal to judge others. In a word, fault finding judgments simply shut off the spigot of God's grace. When we are judgmental, we vainly attempt to take God's place. We decide by our judgments that what matters in life are our standards determined by our limited vision informed by our narrow prejudices fueled by our fickle insecurities. I become the standard for everybody else, hence I can judge everybody else.

Jesus described this malady as an infection of the eye called "log-itis." It is an eye infection caused by a large splintered log or plank protruding from the eye that can cause blurred vision and irritability. Log-itis is a common human problem; it happens all the time. People with a bad case of log-itis tends to walk around picking specks out of everybody else's eyes while clumsily trying to maneuver this huge plank in their own eyes. They don't understand why their vision is blurred and they are irritable.

Critical, judgmental people are to be pitied above all others. The phrase "cutting somebody down to size" is misunderstood. The idea of cutting somebody down to size has been that you are tall, another is short, and you cut them down. A person who is judgmental is given to cutting other people down. Truthfully, a person who cuts others down is actually attempting to cut someone who is higher than they down to their already low level. Show me a person who is judgmental, who has an arrogant, holier-than-thou attitude, and I'll show you a person in whose life self-esteem is very low and the active grace of God is almost nonexistent.

Are you having trouble linking up with God? Do you not understand why your prayers are not going anywhere? Are you not experiencing deep spiritual satisfaction in your life? Don't look up to heaven for some "spiritual" answer. The answer you seek is as near as a judgmental attitude. Take this quiz for yourself and fill in the blank. "I feel superior in the presence of _____" (African Americans? homosexuals? the poor? the uneducated? the unemployed? the obese? the ugly?).[1] Do you want to link up with God? Refuse to be a person infected with log-itis or judgmentalism. The distance you sense from God may be as near as a judgmental attitude.

How do you link up with God? Practice forgiveness. Be a person who practices forgiveness. The Bible reveals from the life of Jesus that forgiveness is not something we fundamentally do as much as it is a reality in which we live. How misguided we are about this. We saunter along in our so-called lives, doing our thing in relationships and work, being with friends, when someone does us wrong. We get our feelings hurt or someone insults us and we get cross with a friend or we are at odds with a family member or a work colleague or a church member. Maybe time passes and we start to feel self-righteous and we say, "You know, I ought to forgive that person. I'll be big about that." And we think that we "do" or practice forgiveness.

Think about that for a moment. "Doing" forgiveness is so foreign to the teachings of Jesus. When our Lord Jesus died on the cross to save the world from its sin, God put a stake in the earth as his Son was raised to the heavens and said, "Forgiveness is not something I will decide on a case-by-case basis. Forgiveness is who I am." So we, who are the sons and daughters of God, are called to live in the reality of forgiveness. "Forgive," said Jesus, "and you will be forgiven."

My beloved teacher who is now with God, Dr. Frank Stagg, opened this verse for me one day in a Greek class. He said, "Look at that phrase." We looked at it in the Greek language. "The verb 'to forgive' is the verb *apheimi* in Greek. It also means to release or 'to set free.' Translate the verse as 'release' instead of 'forgive.'" So we did. "Release, and you will be released."

Show me a person in whose life the reality of forgiveness is not operative and happening on a regular basis, and I will show you a person who is caught in the grip of an unforgiving spirit. They are bound tighter than you can possibly imagine. But witness a person who is living in the reality of forgiveness and they are released, they are free, they are allowing the grace of God to flow through their life.

If forgiveness is not present in our lives, we would be wise to ask ourselves hard questions like "Where is Jesus? Have I accepted my own forgiveness? Do I know myself to be a forgiven person? What may be unresolved in my life? Am I dealing with some issues inappropriately, refusing to face them in the light of the forgiving grace of God?"

The story is told of a farmer who took his two dogs to town every weekend. One was a black dog. One was a white dog. He took them to town to fight every weekend. Sometimes the black dog would win and sometimes the white dog would win. The farmer and spectators would always bet on the dogs, and the dog the farmer bet on always won. After people noticed this for a while, they asked him, "How are you able to choose which dog wins every week?" The farmer said, "It's simple. I feed one and I don't feed the other. The one I feed wins."[2] You can say what you want about forgiveness, but in our lives there is a white dog and a black dog. One of those dogs is called resentment, disappointment, or fear, and the other dog is called forgiveness. The one we feed wins.

Peter had a problem with this. Remember? He came to our Lord one day and said, "If my brother sins against me, should I forgive him seven times?" He thought he was being generous by saying seven. Jesus said, "Peter, not seven, but seventy times seven" (Matt 18:21-22). Jesus meant that forgiveness has no limit. In other words, "Peter, if you are counting the number of times you are going to forgive, you have already missed the message." We are not talking about quantifying a reality. We are talking about a reality in which we live like the air we breathe. We who are the sons and daughters of God live in an atmosphere of the reality of grace and forgiveness. Either we are living in it or we are not.

You say, "What about the person who will not be reconciled to me, what do I do with that?" I know something about that and many of you do, too. I'm thinking about an individual right now with whom I have tried to reconcile for years. I've written a letter. I've made phone calls. I've run into the individual in town, and it is absolutely a shut door. I've tried and it is not that I am so good; I'm not. I have messed up, and I'm sure I have wounded this person, but I can't seem to make it right, and I'm at an impasse. I know how it feels to attempt reconciliation and get nowhere. What do you do? For one thing, you pray. For another, you refuse to demonize the other person. You live with an attitude of surprise, that maybe God would work in amazing ways and reconciliation would take place.

Are you having trouble linking up with God? Don't reach into the air thinking the answer is in some pious place, off on a mountaintop. Don't put your money down on a retreat at the coast. Don't spend your cash on another seminar. It may be as close as an unforgiving heart.

How do you link up with God? Jesus said, "Give and it will be given to you." Be a giver. I don't know why it is, but there are some folks who seem to find giving affirmation and encouragement almost impossible. I have watched children through the years who have grown up under my pastorate. These individuals work, try, and strive, and every time they look in the direction of mom and dad, the look back is never quite enough. The kid hits a double and Dad says, "If you had just lowered the bat a little it could have been a home run." The son runs for 50 yards and almost scores a touchdown and Mom shouts, "If you had just noticed that guy to your left, you could have gone on in for the touchdown!" I've noticed adults who simply cannot seem to affirm another person. The only thing I can attribute it to is that they have not had anybody to show them how to do it. If we want to link up with God, there is a degree to which you and I must become givers of affirmation and acceptance.

We must also become givers of our financial resources. Most church members do not give of their financial resources to the degree God asks. In study after study, across any number of years, Americans give less than 3 percent of their income to any charity (which includes churches). In almost every church, 20 percent of the people give 80 percent of the financial resources. Many church members give nothing or next to nothing year after year. In the last church I served, more than 20 percent of church member families gave nothing to God's work through the church where they had their membership.

Kathie and I have discovered that giving is central to Christian living. Yet, vast numbers of active church members find little or no motivation to give even a token amount, much less a tenth of their income. If you are frustrated and struggling with whether or not you are linking up with God, whether you are connecting with God, you may simply need to look at your checkbook. Your distance from God might be as close as your checkbook. Jesus is right. Only to the degree we give do we discover the power of giving. It may be the giving of financial resources for you. Some of us may be giving liberally financially, but we are falling behind in giving encouragement, hope, and praise. For some, it is easier to write a check than to give time in God's service.

One of the hard things for busy people is giving their presence. That is one of the areas where I struggle. In almost every direction on the compass I turn, somebody wants my attention. It is hard to focus on the one who wants it now. Maybe you struggle with that, too. You want to link up with God? Be a giver. I came across a story recently titled "The Person Down the Road." This is what is says: Every one of us ten, twenty, thirty years from now, if we are fortunate, will meet a person down the road. That person has opportunities every single day to fashion who and what he or she will be. If we are takers, self-centered, and selfish, the person down the road will be crabby, self-centered, selfish, and petty. If we are givers, think of others, and giving to others, the person that we meet down the road will be a giving person. They will be generous and self-giving. You see, the person you will meet down the road is you. And every single day of your life, you are fashioning the person you will be ten or twenty or thirty years from now.[3]

Being spiritual is not a mountaintop, ethereal, otherworldly reality. Fundamentally hooking up with God is earthy. It is reaching out to others with the love of Christ without being judgmental. It is practicing and living in the reality called forgiveness. It is giving generously and faithfully.

Isn't it funny how we search heaven and earth to link up with God? We go here. We read this. We listen to that. We travel the length and breadth of the Christian world looking for the needed connection with God that may be as near as a judgmental attitude. It may be as close as an unforgiving heart. It may be as touchable as your checkbook.

How do I link up with God? How do I experience forgiveness? How do I walk deeply in the Spirit? My friend, put your feet on earth and listen to what Jesus said. If you do these things, you will be amazed at how the God connection will change you.

[1] I am grateful to Dr. Ron Bradley of First Baptist Church, Roswell, Georgia, for the substance of this test.

[2] I am indebted to Dr. Gary Carver of First Baptist Church, Chattanooga, Tennessee, for this story.

[3] Ibid.

Stones for Bread

Is there anyone among you who, if your child asks for bread, will give a stone? — Matthew 7:9

I am haunted by Jesus' question: "If your child asks for bread, will you give him a stone?" That's outrageous, ludicrous, some would even say abusive. You would report a father who responded to his son or daughter's hunger in such a way. Yet the analogy is obvious if you have been to the land of the Bible. There, you see far more stones than loaves of bread. In fact, everywhere you look in the Middle East, you see thousands of acres of land covered with stones.

Perhaps we need to rethink the question and put it in different words. Maybe Jesus was saying, "Which one of you, having a child who asks for that which might require your resources, your work, your care, your compassion, would instead give the child something picked up off the ground—anything that was handy, the nearest, easiest thing?" Who in the world would do something like that?

Who would treat a child that way? Imagine a five-year-old child asking in hunger for bread and the father giving the child a rock. Who would do that? I stand here this morning to say we all do it all the time.

It has been one of those draining days. Dads and Moms, you know what I'm talking about, don't you? It has been one of those days when your life seems like a big laundry tub and you have been going down the middle part of the drain. Your customers haven't been satisfied, nothing has gone right, the office situation has not been good. It's been this and that between a couple of coworkers. You've had enough of that kind of thing all day long. It's been one of those draining, difficult days.

When you pull into the driveway of your home, you look up and your wide-eyed daughter runs with joy to your open arms. In a moment of absolute insanity, you turn her away, or worse, ignore her invitation to play. You simply don't have energy for a six-year-old this late in the afternoon after your exhausting day. She runs to greet you needing bread, and you give her a stone.

Couples do this all the time. It is a real marriage killer. A wife in desperate need of a listening ear and the husband locked into a Martian cave.[1] A husband needing some passion, a wife too self-absorbed in her demanding life to reciprocate. Both husband and wife needing bread and yet giving each other stones. "Which of you, if his son asks for bread, will give him a stone?"

It gives me no joy to report that we do this unconsciously around the church all too often. Guests walk through church doors unnoticed. Sometimes they are ignored or if welcomed, they are not nurtured, guided, or informed. They are not warmly received and brought into the church fellowship in a caring, genuine way. That doesn't happen often in most churches, but when it does, a person needing bread is given a cold stone.

It can happen in Sunday school classes; hurting people are sitting in class with you, and others have been absent for weeks and never contacted. They are hurting people out in the trenches of life going through a difficult time, and no one from the class happens to notice or even ask, "Where has 'so-and-so' been the last four or five weeks?" Needing bread, given stones.

I've been preaching from pulpits for nearly thirty years. As I wrote this sermon, I was sobered to think about the hundreds of sermons I've preached and the number of times people walked into the church, sat down for the service needing bread, and received only a lifeless, inanimate rock from me. They needed bread. They needed nourishment. They needed strength. And I gave them rocks. Jesus' question has disturbed me for a long time.

What do we do with this? The truth is we are all so forgetful. We forget. We dress up on a Sunday morning in our Sunday best. We put on the Sunday costume. Whether we are in church or in the business place, the office, the classroom, or wherever we are doing our thing, the situation is the same. We think it's important to convince everybody that we have it all together, that everything is okay, even as we forget how ravenously hungry we are. No job, no title, no income, no fine clothing, no good neighborhood, no locked tight security system can satisfy that hunger.

Not long ago, I "starved" my way through a book written by the Polish writer Slavomir Rawicz, *The Long Walk*. The book is Rawicz's story about his life as a Polish cavalry officer who in 1939 was fighting the Germans when they invaded Poland. He retreated across Poland to the Russian border and happened to cross the Russian border, where the Russians arrested him for being a spy. He was put through the justice system of Josef Stalin's Soviet Union and sentenced to twenty-five years of hard labor in Siberia. After a 2,500-mile train ride in a cattle car east across Russia into Siberia, he was forced to walk the last 1,000 miles in the winter, chained to the back of a truck.

His daily ration was two cups of coffee and a loaf of bread. I tell you I starved through the whole book. Rawicz finally escaped from Gulag #303 and walked with a small group of men 3,000 miles to India and freedom. Reading *The Long Walk* reminded me how hungry human beings can get physically and spiritually. I am convinced we are not in touch with our own spiritual hunger. When another asks us for bread, we don't know what to do. Our forgetfulness contributes to our being insensitive, to giving stones for bread. I suspect that is what Jesus had in mind when he spoke the best-known words he uttered. We know it as "the Golden Rule." You find it in Matthew 7:12. I wonder why our Lord followed his "stones-for-bread" saying with "the Golden Rule"?

Perhaps the Golden Rule—"So in everything do unto others what you would have them do unto you"—reminds us that we need to get in touch with this hungry side of ourselves so that when people around us ask for bread, we don't give them stones.

Right now there are people sharing the pew with you in your church, even during the high hour of worship at eleven o'clock on a Sunday morning—you might even be one of them—who are starving inside. They would never let you know it because all too often they have come to folks like us asking for bread and we have given them stones. They are sure not going to ask for bread on a Sunday morning. It is easy to come into a worship service where much bread is offered— music, Scripture, sermon, fellowship, warm bodies around us—and miss the bread. Let me be fair. There are times in all of our lives when God offers us bread and we throw it down like a stone. God comes to us with awesome grace. God comes with forgiveness and hope, and what do we do? Do we listen, experience, and receive the grace gifts of God as bread? Sometimes. But often, too often, we throw them down as if they are stones.

In times of loss and sorrow we pick up the Bible and read that life-giving line from Jesus who said, "I am the resurrection and the life." But in our sorrow, our bitterness, our loss we throw it down like so many rocks. An article in *USA Today* reported some time ago that people sixty-four years of age and older who attended religious services were 46 percent less likely to die over a six-year period than those who did not attend services. I don't know what that says to you, but I would come to church more often. What it says to me is that in the context of a worship service, in an hour like this, with ordinary people like us, right here in this moment, there is the obvious possibility that God is nourishing us and giving us spiritual bread. Still, so often we wad the service up and throw it on the floor, saying as we make our way to a hot car, "Now that church is over, I need a tee time at 1:15." Given bread, we throw it down as a stone.

What does this mean for a church? At the least, it means we would be wise to be more intentional about giving and receiving bread in our common life. If we deeply believed that the baking and giving of bread was at the heart of our mission, we would be more intentional about using our Sunday School for its intended purpose, which is to teach the Bible and to create small, caring relational groups where the truths of the Bible are applied to life. We would serve more bread.

Sunday school teachers, when your class gathers every Sunday, whether they are preschoolers or children, youth or young adults, median or senior adults, wherever they are on the life spectrum, if you are a Sunday School teacher, please, in God's name, give bread not stones. Don't come to your senses between your toast and coffee on Sunday morning and say, "What do I teach today? I guess I'll just get by," and throw out a stone to the class. Class members, when your fellow learners are ripped apart by life that is often cruel and unforgiving, please, in God's name, give bread to the people in the class with you.

A church is the body of Christ, the people of God. We have a simple mission. We are to share the love of God in Jesus Christ. We are called to be givers of bread in a hungry, needy world. We are to grow nurturing, loving, and encouraging people as Jesus encourages us.

I've served five churches. I've been in dozens of churches as a guest preacher. I've read about churches the better part of twenty-five years in the ministry. I read a lot about what churches are doing. Most churches—small or large—are well organized to keep the institution of the church going. We know how to oil the institutional machinery of the church. We have the organizational chart down. But where we must be diligent, where we must become absolutely convicted and focused is in organizing the heart. We must be organized to love and nurture people who walk through our doors whether they are members or strangers, saved or lost. All who come to us looking for bread must never be given stones. We must offer bread.

Several years ago in another church I served as pastor, I visited with a woman who was literally hard-wired into the foundation of that church. Just like they weld steel rods into the foundation of a building, this lady was welded into the church. Her family had been there for generations. She confided in me about a difficult time she was having in her life and the brokenness in her family. My heart went out to her. After I listened for a while, I asked her, "Tell me, have you shared this with your Sunday school class?" She answered quickly, her eyes flashing, "Oh, I could never do that. What would they think of me if I told them this story?" I thought to myself, here is a woman who has received so many stones when she asked for bread that she is not about to ask again. "Which of you, if his son asks for bread will give him a stone?"

I have a habit of keeping the bread that is passed my way. I throw the stones away. I would highly recommend doing that. When someone gives you bread, keep it. When somebody offers you a stone, throw it away. It's not worth keeping. I rediscovered a letter I had tucked away in a little book. It came my way almost seventeen years ago. It's the only letter I have that my paternal grandmother wrote to me. I wish you could have known my grandmother. She died in 1989, a week before Christmas in her ninety-seventh year. The only night she ever spent in the hospital was the night she died. I am so glad I've got those genes. She played ragtime piano music, played for the silent movie theaters, entertained our family so many times. I had forgotten how much bread was in this note. I would like to read it to you. You will have to excuse my grandmother; she is given to excess. When I received this letter, my son Nathan was eight, Justin was six, and Lindsey was five.

Dear Tim, There is not one thing I can say about you, but you are a wonderful good man. As your grandmother, I have been with you for lots of your life, and you was always grand and sweet. Tim, I'm so proud of you and appreciate you. You are a wonderful husband, good father, and a good preacher. I have heard you preach several times, and no one is better. [I told you she got a little carried away.] I hope to see you soon and to hear you preach. Lots of love, Mamma T

You know how long a loaf of bread can feed a soul? Some of you need to write a letter to your church's youth minister, even if you don't have teenagers and haven't had them around your house for twenty years, and tell that minister what a good job he or she is doing. Others of you who haven't had babies around the house for such a long time that you've forgotten what a diaper is need to write a note to one of the faithful people who work in the preschool ministry of your church keeping the little ones. Tell that person what a good job he or she is doing with our preschoolers and children. Give bread.

Some of you need to write your Sunday School teacher, who for thirty years or more has been opening the word of God and feeding your soul, while not once have you taken the time to drop him or her a note and say, "Thank you." Teenagers, learn how to use your hand and write. Write to people who have blessed your life. Give bread. It will not be thrown away.

It's kind of ridiculous, isn't it? "Which of you, if his son asks for bread, will give him a stone?" People of God, please, in God's name, give bread.

<hr/>

[1] The "cave," popularized by John Gray in his book *Men Are from Mars, Women Are from Venus*, is the place to which males retreat to sort out their problems in solitude.

The Robbed among Us

A man was going down from Jerusalem to Jericho.
—Luke 10:30

The parable of the Good Samaritan may be the most misnamed story Jesus told, but the naming has stuck. In fact, across the centuries, hospitals, orphanages, shelters, and hospices have been named for this nameless "good guy" traveling the road between Jerusalem and Jericho. Its popularity notwithstanding, I wonder if we have we missed the bite, the sting of the story. What if the hero in the story, as one commentator suggests, is not the Samaritan but the bruised and half-dead lump of a man in the ditch, the loser mugged, robbed, and left for dead? What if we have read the tale and been so conditioned to place the spotlight on the Samaritan that we have missed the real center of the story?

Robert Farrar Capon reminds us that this parable is not told "to teach us the saving truth about the power of human niceness."[1] This is not a story about niceness, nor is it a story about doing good. If it is not that, then what is it? Capon may be on to something here. He delights in taking the parables of Jesus and turning them every way but predictable. Let's go with his suggestion and see where it takes us.

Look at the man in the ditch. Focus on the "ditch dweller," the robbed man. I know it is tough to hear a story in a new way when it is hard-wired to our souls. Even so, I urge you to look at the man in the ditch. What if at some place, in some way, all of us here today are in the ditch dying, bleeding, half-dead/half-alive, waiting for someone, anyone, to stoop down where we are and lift us up?

The truth is that the mugged, the beaten, the half-dead may be in your skin right now. You may attend a church, pick up the Bible from time to time, even do acts of devotion. But it all seems for naught because, for one thing, you simply cannot pray. It is not that you are mad at God, and it is surely not because you don't want to pray. It is not that you don't have the words. No, the words are there, but your soul is too scarred and your dreams have been twisted. Something or several somethings have happened in recent days to shut down your soul. Neither the motivation nor the language is alive in your being to pray.

I suspect there are others who have lost the ability even to feel. You are numbed. Your soul has been anesthetized by the cruelties of life. I think there are more than a few of us who are afraid to love, to give, to be vulnerable to anybody, even God. You say, "Christian people? In a church? I don't know anyone like that." Really? I beg to differ. We could not be in the human family and not be numbered at some time among the robbed.

Often the person who has been mugged and robbed is a stranger, a guest, a new face in your church or Bible study class. All of us who worship with others in a church somewhere would be wise to keep asking ourselves if the congregation of which we are a part is hospitable to the robbed who walk through the doors. I am not talking about the temperature of the room or the cleanliness of the buildings. I am not asking whether the rest rooms are clean, the chairs properly arranged, or the Bible study/devotional material readily available. That is not what I'm talking about. I'm asking whether we are in touch with the fact that people who walk through our doors, who are our guests, who may be strangers, didn't just wake up in the morning and say, "You know, I ought to go to church today. That would be a nice thing to do." I believe many people who walk through our doors "claw" their way through the outward, imposing structure of the our church buildings and parking lots. Afraid, they make their way to church because a robbery has taken place in their hearts. Desperate, they are at a place in their lives where they think that maybe the people in the church would care for their souls.

You say, "I don't think I get where you are going here. Our church members are friendly people." Let me tell you a story. I was having lunch a couple of years ago with a couple who had recently joined our church. The man is a naturally gregarious, outgoing person, not a retiring, wallpaper personality. He and his wife came to Sunday School and, with careful words, made this observation to me. "If we had not literally pushed ourselves into the center of that Sunday School class's circle, we would have never gotten in." I said, "What do you mean?" He said, "You know what I mean. In every group there is an invisible circle of relationships and friends. It is not that they are not happy to see us or don't want to include us. Rather, they are managing so many relationships already, we are just one more to have to manage. We simply had to push ourselves into that group."

Hear me carefully. Every Christian can be intentional and aware in touching, looking, reaching out, creating eye contact, and offering a warm handshake hard-wired to a caring face. One hand is extended toward a well-known friend and the other hand is looking for the new person needing care, compassion, and ministry. Why? Because many folks who walk through our church doors, who may be strangers in our midst, finally find the courage somewhere in their souls to say, "I need the fellowship of a Christian church. I have been robbed. I want to find God and myself again." This is one of the primary responsibilities of the church—to care for the robbed among us.

We sing it. "I was lost but Jesus found me." The robbed are among us. In fact, wherever you turn your head you will find the robbed among us: Children who live surrounded more by conflict than love or who grow up under the stinging lash of criticism rather than the outstretched hand of grace. The divorced who feel as if, because of that failure in a relationship, they must somehow find a way to get reconnected with God, the church, and others, all the while feeling as if they are wearing the big "D" on their chest. The grieving who know the brutal lash of being robbed—the loss of physical vitality, professional identity, family configuration.

Hurting people know the helplessness that comes from being robbed by loss. Our young people are struggling with this issue. Young people who have abandoned innocence because they live in a world with too much violence and too little vision, too many sexual pressures and too few spiritual companions. The robbed are among us, and yes, they are among us every Lord's Day as we gather in some place for worship.

But truth to tell, I suspect the most overlooked victim of life's robberies is the one right inside our own skin. We are mugged by guilt over something that is long past but continually returns as a primetime rerun in our lives. Bloodied by family strife, left half-dead, half-alive by messages heard in childhood that cannot seemingly be erased. "You are slow." "You are awkward." "You are lazy." "When are you ever going to amount to anything?" "Don't you know if you don't work hard all the time you will be considered slothful, lazy, and good for nothing?" We grow up with these messages that rob us of whole dimensions of our humanity, and only God can put them back in our lives.

I know men and women who are sixty, seventy years of age and older who cannot redirect their life's energy. Why? Because they got an early message when they were six or seven that said, "You have to work all your life, or you will never amount to anything and people will think you are lazy." I know young people who have grown up under such incredible, unforgiving criticism that they almost wilt, not believing that God has placed within their lives incredible resources and gifts. A few years ago, the cover story of *Newsweek* dealt with the college entrance examination known as the SAT. If you are taking it or going to take it, or you have a child who is going to take it, you know the stress created just by the thought of taking that test. The issue dealt with the debate about testing our children. I am not against testing. You have to test. But I am against fixating on some number generated by a test, scored by a computer, that puts a value on a human life. Such nonsense perpetrates grand larceny on a human destiny.

Is there any hope for us? The story is clear that religion is of little or no help. A priest is going down the road, leaving his duties at the temple in Jerusalem. A Levite is coming up that same road to do his work at the temple. Religion goes up and down the road, passing by with no help. But a Samaritan shows up. He not only applies first aid, but he also depletes his bank account to set us up at a fine hotel with room service, all paid for, no questions asked.

My friend, this is the picture of God, not of some "do-gooder" organization. This is the picture of God who shows up as an outcast, a spendthrift paying for everything we need with the currency of a bloody cross, a borrowed tomb, and an empty grave. This is not a parable about niceness or being nice. Rather, it is a story about facing the fact that we have been robbed. We are terminal, beat up, and left for dead unless the spendthrift God comes and saves us. In a word, this is not about the power of human niceness, but the power of divine grace.

Don't get me wrong. Who doesn't want to be thought of as nice? But when you're robbed and left in the ditch to die alone, nice is the last thing you need. In truth, when robbed, you want to be alive. And only God can do that.

We have misnamed this parable. This is not the parable about the Good Samaritan suggesting we are all to be Samaritans in our work and in our world. That may be an important thing to do, but it's another story. I don't see it here. This is a story about the likes of you and me who are traveling the road of life, who inevitably get beat up, mugged, and left for dead without hope until God comes. God comes in a spendthrift, reckless way in Jesus Christ to pick our bloodied mess of a life up out of the ditch, spending all God has, even God's only Son to give us life and a future.

Look around you today. Remember Yogi Berra? "You can observe a lot by looking around." Look around, but in God's name, don't forget to look within. If you look carefully and listen attentively, you will find that somewhere, somehow, you either are, were, or will be headed for a ditch from which only grace can save you. That is the message of Jesus. "For God so loved the world, he gave his only Son, that whosoever believes in him should not perish but have everlasting life."

Who doesn't want to be nice and thought of as nice? What all of us may need far more than niceness is to be made alive. Only God can do that.

[1] Robert Farrar Capon, *The Parables of Grace* (Grand Rapids: William B. Eerdmans Publishing Company, 1988), 63.

Risky Business

Rabbi, who sinned, this man or his parents,
that he was born blind?
—John 9:2

Psychiatrist M. Scott Peck dashed by a thought in a book he wrote several years ago that will not leave me alone. When I read the book, this observation hooked me; it still bounces around in the walls of my mind. In substance, Dr. Peck said that the most courageous people he knew were people in therapy. That surprised me. I didn't think the most courageous people in the world were those in therapy. I thought the most courageous people in the world were people in the military or people battling cancer or people dealing with some kind of brokenness. And then it hit me. He's right. The most courageous people are those who know they have deep, scarring, crippling wounds and yet choose to get help. For Dr. Peck, they are life's heroes, courageous beyond words.[1]

By that definition, I believe everyone who attends and/or participates in Christian worship is courageous beyond words. Heroic might be a better word. Think about it. No one requires an adult to show up at a church somewhere and worship God. Come to think of it, you can sit in a church and check out mentally. Some do. By the fact that you are reading this book, I suspect you are a courageous person. You choose to engage in the spiritual journey. You don't have to do so, but you are. When you attend a worship service, you hear the Scripture and sing the hymns because something in you longs to be addressed by God. Somewhere in the depths of your being you know you have a need only God can meet. You, my friend, are more courageous than you know.

I want us to think about this courage for the next little while. I would couch our conversation with this question: What risks are you willing to take to change the rest of your life? I'm talking risky business here. What courageous, heroic risk are you willing to take to change the rest of your life?

Jesus was walking along with his disciples somewhere in the city of Jerusalem when they came upon a man who was blind from birth. His world was veiled in ominous darkness. He could hear, speak, laugh, sing, walk, touch, taste, smell, and, yes, he knew all too well human hurt. But he could not see. He was blind from birth; thick darkness draped his entire life. The disciples looked at the man as did Jesus and quickly thought they would use him as a springboard into a theological conversation.

Don't be too hard on the disciples. We do what they did all the time. "Preacher, tell me, what about that person who took his or her own life? Is there hope for them in the next life?" (Let me say absolutely. God's grace reaches even those whose pain leads them to take their own lives.) You know what we do? Just like Jesus' disciples, we dehumanize people with theological and philosophical prattle. We deal with the "what ifs" and "what abouts" and "perhaps." But there before our Lord and his disciples was a real, live, breathing human being with deep needs.

Jesus refused to devalue him. Did you notice how Jesus answered their question? I suppose I have read this text dozens of times. I wrote a doctoral dissertation on the Gospel of John. I have read through the Gospel front to back and back to front. I've preached on this text many times. Verses 3 and 4 have always bothered me and I couldn't understand why until several years ago. As I was reading a state Baptist newspaper, I came across an article by the late Dr. Herschel Hobbs in which he lifted out these two verses for commentary. When I read it, I clipped it out and put it in my file. It is now yellowed because I have had it for so long.

For the first time, Dr. Hobbs made sense of what I thought were senseless verses. Quite frankly, as they were translated in the King James and New International versions, I didn't like them; they did not sound like the Jesus I knew from the rest of the Gospels. Here again is the NIV translation of John 9:3-4: "The disciples asked Jesus, 'Rabbi, who sinned, this man or his parents, that he was born blind?' 'Neither this man nor his parents sinned,' said Jesus, 'but this happened so that the work of God might be displayed in his life.'"

I never liked that. I didn't contract polio at thirteen months of age so that God could display God's works in me. You don't get cancer so God can display God's works in you. We don't serve a God like that. I don't worship a God like that. I never did like the theology of those two verses.

According to Dr. Hobbs, the problem with these verses is that we have allowed later editors to tell us how to punctuate them. Did you know that in the ancient Greek there were no commas, no periods, no colons, no semicolons? There were no punctuation marks. In fact, the words weren't even separated. The recorders simply lined up the letters, and all the words ran together. Editors have come along through the ages to separate words and add punctuation. Let me ask you to do what Dr. Hobbs suggests. Take your Bible and look at it. Before the word "but" in verse 3, add a period. Then we will keep reading the whole sentence into verse 4. Here is the Owings translation: "'Neither this man sinned nor his parents,' said Jesus. 'But that the works of God might be manifested in him, I must work the works of him who sent me while it is day, for night is coming when no man can work.'" That puts a totally different wrinkle on it. "Neither this man sinned nor his parents. But that the works of God might be manifest in him—that the works of God might be manifest in you!—I must work the works of him who sent me while it is day. For night is coming when no one can work." What does this mean? Jesus is working to bring light, life, and sight to you and me now. The question is: Are we willing to let Christ do his work in us?

I think about the man who was asked, "Do you want to live forever?" "I don't know about that," he said. "I do know I want to live for real."[2] That's where we all are. We pose salvation questions in terms of forever and the "by and by," when in the depths of our being we are asking, "Could we live for real now?"

I have a hunch. Maybe you could "hunch it" with me. My hunch is this: Most of us believe hypothetical lives are a safe escape from the real stuff we have to deal with day after day. Think about the success of sitcoms and soap operas. The lure, the narcotic, the fascination with fictitious, hypothetical lives captures so many, while they ignore their real lives, histories, relationships, dreams, futures. So we ask, "What about?" and "What if?" We peer and leer into the television at sitcoms or we pick up the tabloids and read about people "out there" while ignoring the real people around us, even ourselves. We deal with hypothetical life rather than real life.

I want to do some real-life thinking with you for a moment. Two things. First—in the "let's be candid" category—is this: It's risky business to believe Jesus Christ can make you well, now, today, here. Baptists talk about accepting Jesus as our personal Savior. Why do we do that? Because God respects, loves, and values each of us so much. God longs to relate to us at the intimate, interior level of our lives. God says, "I want to deal with your real life. You are a real person. I respect you so much. I choose to relate to you." But it is risky to relate to God. On the one hand, we in the church can talk safely about theories, philosophies, and theologies. We sit in our safe Sunday School classes, open our safe Bibles, even come in and out of church week after week and deal with theoretical, even abstract faith and not let God do God's work by the Spirit in our heart of hearts.

This is risky business because the risky step of faith, the risky step of believing, says that I am better off in relationship with God than I am without God. I don't know whether you believe that, but I do. I believe that I am better off in relationship with God than I would be without God.

Almost thirty years ago, I asked Kathie Pignato to marry me. At that moment we were greener than the green silk arrangements that adorn most altars in our churches. I asked her to marry me and surprisingly she said, "Yes." The reason I asked her to marry me, and I would do it all over again today, is because I believed and she believed that our tomorrows would be better in relationship with each other than all of our yesterdays.

You ask me why I am a Christian. At a much deeper, more significant, ultimate level, I believe my life is infinitely better with Jesus Christ than it would be without Christ. But if you think it is a safe move, if you think it is some kind of safe spiritual move to believe, think again. Look at this blind man. Here he is with mud on his face, fumbling, stumbling, groping through the narrow streets of Jerusalem, moving down, down, down to the Pool of Siloam, there to wash his face and discover sight.

You ask, "Was it risky?" From all appearances, it was plain stupid. But he took the step of faith, risky as it was, and God changed his darkened, blind life with life-changing power. Are you willing to take such a risk with Christ?

It is risky business to believe this Jesus Christ saves and changes us, but hear me. It is far riskier to try to do life on our own. Oh, yes, it's risky to take the step of faith. We all come to the precipice and wonder, "Can I leap into the arms of God and trust God with my life?" Yes, you can. But know this: it's infinitely riskier to move back into the darkness and think, "I can handle life on my own."

Look at the blind man again. How was he handling life without Christ? He was handling life by begging. That was his life before he met Jesus, blind and begging. It dawned on me not long ago that we're all like that without Christ. We can see all right. We can enjoy the beauty of stained-glass windows, the glory of the coming spring, the loving expression of a husband or wife, the dimpled cheeks of a newborn baby. Mind you, we can see. But without Jesus Christ, we are always begging for someone else's experience, begging for another's understanding of God, another's sight or insight, another's light, all the while never understanding that God would give us life and light if only we would ask. It is risky to believe. It is far riskier to think, "I can handle it on my own, thank you."

When he died, he had served the longest tenure of any mayor in the United States. He was the mayor of our town in south Florida. He had been reelected, reelected, and reelected. I think for between forty and fifty years he had served as mayor. He was a meat cutter, a butcher. So many times he had run unopposed, because, quite frankly, who would ever go up against the mayor?

When the man was in his eighties after being hospitalized, my pastor learned that he had come home. So he said to himself, "I'm going over and talk to the mayor about his relationship to God." Everybody in town knew he was not a churchman; few knew anything about a Christian commitment. My pastor called him. He went over to see him. When he went into his house, he found the mayor up a ladder changing a light bulb. He began to talk with the mayor, a man financially wealthy and politically connected. As I said, he held the record at that time for the longest-running leadership as mayor in a major metropolitan city. My pastor went to his home to talk with him about Jesus Christ.

As he told the story to me, after talking with the mayor and asking him to give his life to Jesus, he said, "Tim, he looked at me, held out his cupped hands and this is what he said. 'Preacher, all my life I've taken care of myself with these two hands.'" Now in his eighties, he continued, "And when it comes to the next life I'll just handle it the way I'm handling this one." In a matter of a few weeks he was dead.

I don't know where you are in the risky business of doing life. Maybe you think you can handle life on your own. Maybe from all the external signs you are doing pretty well. But if you are like me, you know deep down in your soul that you need a relationship with God that can make you different from the inside out. It is risky to believe. It is far riskier to try it on your own. Jesus says, "I have come to give you sight." My friend, you can believe this Jesus.

---

[1] M. Scott Peck, M.D., makes this observation throughout his provocative book about his spiritual awakening at mid-life (*In Search of Stones: A Pilgrimage of Faith, Reason, and Discovery* [New York: Simon & Schuster, 1996]).

[2] From an article by Dr. George Mason, Pastor of Wilshire Baptist Church, Dallas, Texas.

How Narrow?

Strive to enter through the narrow door.
—Luke 13:24

We do not sing this hymn as often as did our foreparents, but its power sings across the generations. "There's a wideness in God's mercy like the wideness of the sea, There's a kindness in his justice which is more than liberty; But we make his love too narrow by false limits of our own, And we magnify his strictness with a zeal he will not own." How narrow is narrow? "For we make his love too narrow with a zeal he will not own." But how narrow?

Baptists and other traditions with revivalistic roots have not fared well in the court of public opinion. Through the years, long before this generation, Baptists were called narrow-minded, obtuse, thick-headed. Baptists have had our share of licks on being narrow. I remember when I was growing up it was said that Baptist preachers were so narrow you could sleep four of them in a twin bed.

How narrow does narrow have to be? Jesus said, "Strive to enter through the narrow door; for many, I tell you, will try to enter and will not be able." Matthew has another memory, perhaps of another day, another sermon, another audience, another group to whom Jesus said, "Enter through the narrow gate; for the gate is wide and the road is easy that leads to destruction, and there are many who take it. For the gate is narrow and the road is hard that leads to life, and there are few who find it" (Matt 7:13-14). How narrow is narrow?

Jesus is on the road to Jerusalem, the road to suffering, the road to death. Some unnamed someone tosses him a question. "Lord, will only a few be saved?" That is a question every preacher hears. Young people like this question. Adults pitch the question a little bit differently. The man in the crowd said, "Lord, will only a few be saved?" Our question is, "What about the heathen in some remote, out-of-the-way place that, of course, we would never visit, say like the Amazon of Africa?" That's a safe question: "What about them?" Look carefully at Jesus' answer to the man. He asked, "What about them?" Jesus said, in so many words, "What about you? "*You* [emphasis mine] strive to enter through the narrow door." For there will come a time when the owner will shut the door and *you* will stand outside and knock at the door and *you* will say, "Lord, open to us." Then he will say to *you*, "I do not know where *you* come from."

Here is an answer to the question we didn't bargain for. Granted we are all curious. There is something about the human makeup, the human mind, the DNA of the human imagination that longs to peer into the future and wonder, What about them? Jesus looks all of us square in the eye and says, "You enter by the narrow door." There is something here we may not be prepared to face. How narrow is narrow?

Jesus' response to this unnamed man in the crowd deals with what may be the number one sin of good people, the sin of presumption, of entitlement, of position. We, of course, are the ones who have made it. We are the ones who have entered the kingdom of God. What about them? Do you see it? Here is a presumptive question that smacks of entitlement, of inside information, of membership, of those who have arrived wanting to know about those whom we believe have not yet arrived and may, in our limited judgment, never arrive. Here is a question "insiders" ask about the "outsiders."

We hear it in the text, don't we? Again, if I may paraphrase Jesus: "There is coming a time when the door is shut and you will raise the protest saying, 'Excuse me, didn't we invite you to dinner at our house? Didn't our mayor arrange for you to speak to the big crowd at the town square? I thought we were the ones who took care of you.'" Jesus looks through the eyes of the man on the inside, the host of the meal, and says, "I do not know where you come from. There will come a day at a great banquet when Abraham and Isaac and Jacob and all the prophets will be in the kingdom of God, but you will be thrown out" (Luke 13:26-28).

This is not a warm, fuzzy story. In fact, I don't like it any more than you do. It is not the kind of thing we want to turn over in our minds as we sit down for a relaxing Sunday afternoon with the paper and remember warm, winsome, charming reflections on the sermon. How narrow is narrow? "Try to enter by the narrow door."

I have not done well with this text. I have wrestled it to the ground. I have put a hammerlock on it. I have gone to other minds. I have come to one conclusion only to be swayed by another. As a preacher, times are you give title and text to a sermon thinking "I think I'll go there." And then, finally, you get there and say, "What in the world am I doing here?" What in the world is Jesus talking about here? How narrow?

I can only come up with two things. The first, for me at least, is that he is talking about a narrow loyalty. There are things about the Christian faith that demand a big reach or a wide embrace. There is a wideness in God's mercy. The hymn writer is right; God's mercy and grace are wide. There are things about the Christian faith that are radically inclusive, accepting, and affirming. Throughout my pastoral ministry, I have been intentional, sometimes painfully so, about being inclusive, accepting, affirming. With all my good intentions, however, I have not batted 1.000.

But there is another side of the gospel coin that cannot be ignored. There is a dimension to our faith that is intensely narrow. I'm thinking this morning of a narrow loyalty particularly to God in Jesus Christ. Quite frankly, there is a ton of baggage we have placed on Jesus that is not Jesus. Today, more than ever in the life of the church, we need a narrow loyalty to Jesus Christ.

Earlier in this thirteenth chapter there is a wonderful but disturbing story about Jesus in a synagogue on the Sabbath day (Luke 13:10-17). Our Lord is in that place of prayer and notices a woman bent over with an infirmity. She has been in that condition for eighteen years. Bible numbers often mean something. Eighteen years equals three times the incomplete number six. Luke may be suggesting she has a triple deficiency, a thrice inflicted pain if not of her body, of her spirit. She has been bent over for eighteen years. But, like every Sabbath, there are services. And yes, the people gather and hear the Bible read. They have prayers and participate in the other elements of worship.

Right in the middle of the service, not in the order of worship, Jesus looks at this woman and says, "You are healed." At that moment, there is an uproar. "Excuse me, that was not in the order of worship. Don't you know this is the Sabbath day? Can't you do your healing on one of the other six days in the week? If you want to put out your shingle and heal people, no problem. But you are not going to do it on the Sabbath, and you are definitely not going to do it here."

Our Lord listened. He was polite. Then he looked at them and said, "You hypocrites! You will take care of the animals on your place, sheep and donkeys. You will do this and that for less than human things, while this daughter of Abraham has been bent over for eighteen years and you don't even see her anymore." What is he saying? In this story we see a system that had made a fundamental decision about this crippled woman. What she was was what she would always be. Then Jesus came to the service. Jesus said, "There is something more important than following all the rules and making sure everything goes just right, and that is the liberation of human beings by the power of God." How narrow? Above all things, a narrow loyalty to our Lord, who is in our midst by his Spirit.

The church has only one Lord and only one gospel. We would be wise to ask a certain question on a regular basis: What is Jesus calling us to be? There must be a narrow loyalty to Jesus entered by the narrow door. Then we say, "Aren't we going down this road of narrow-mindedness we Baptists have always had?" Someone has said that in every endeavor in life where excellence is required, you find a narrow, focused, disciplined commitment to whatever it takes to be number one. How many hours does Tiger Woods practice his putting? You don't see him on the putting surface often, but how many hours does he practice his putting? How many miles does a cross-country cyclist like Lance Armstrong ride every day?

The late Artur Rubenstein was asked once about his practice routine when he was performing piano recitals all over the world. Rubenstein supposedly said, "Well, it's this way. If I don't practice one day, I know it. If I don't practice two days, the critics know it. If I don't practice three days, everybody knows it." There is a loyalty, a focus, a narrowness to many aspects of life. Life in its fullness and wonder requires some degree of discipline, focus, and attention. How narrow? For those who traffic in good news, there must be a narrow loyalty to Jesus Christ.

Many wonderful endeavors clamor for our attention in the communities where we live. Human needs are being met through any number of agencies and programs around the globe. I, like you, and our family, like your family, are sensitive to that and try to help where we can. But I know of no loyalty in my life that is greater than my loyalty to Jesus Christ and the people of God. How narrow? Narrowly focused on Jesus Christ.

How narrow? I hear Jesus saying there must be a narrow responsibility. Here we have the heart of the dialogue we overhear in Luke's Gospel. "Lord, will only a few be saved? What about him? What about her? What about them?" Jesus says, "The better question is, 'What about me? What about you?'" We are tempted in our lives to pass wide judgment on others and not face the narrow judgment on ourselves, to debate sterile theological problems while ignoring the weightier matters of practicing compassion, giving grace, being gospel to others. "Enter by the narrow door."

This was the problem the prophet Isaiah raised. In the twenty-eighth chapter of the book that bears his name, Isaiah talks about the people's need to practice compassion, to live out justice, to be a people of righteousness (vv. 14-18). There is a narrow responsibility. I know some folks out there today will say, "What the church needs to do is hold up the ideals of living right, being a Christian, walk the straight and narrow: no dancing, drinking, card playing, cursing, and carousing." Is that it? Is that what we are all about? Is that what narrow means?

At one time I was convinced that was the meaning of the text, but I am not convinced any longer. Narrow behavior? Narrow mind? Narrowness? No, that is not what is going on here. Rather, here is a narrow devotion, a narrow loyalty to Jesus Christ and the responsibilities that come to us when we narrowly say, "I am following Jesus."

How narrow? As narrow as a nail, as narrow as a cross, as narrow as the Savior. How narrow? Only to the degree we are narrowly loyal to Jesus Christ and the responsibilities that come with following Jesus, only to that degree do we wake up to the wideness of God's mercy. Do you see it? It is only when we say "Jesus Christ is Savior and Lord. I am following Jesus" that life finds its highest loyalty, its sacred priorities. Only when you and I give Jesus our narrow loyalty, only then can we discover how wide our lives really become.

Do you know what we do instead? We start off wide and never get to narrow. How does that happen? We take our Christian faith and we see it as one component of what we are defining as "the good life." We have this wide idea that Jesus and the church can be one thing among many things in our lives that are good. The church is like one train car in a line of train cars. So, when it comes to politics, profession, hobby, sports leagues, club memberships, or the using of our financial resources, the church is just one thing, albeit a good thing, in a string of other things in this wide part of our lives.

We wonder why the church is so marginalized in our culture. "Strive to enter the narrow door." If Jesus is the One around whom all of life is ordered, then work and leisure and family and civic responsibilities and a dozen other demands on our lives take on a different weight when we are narrowly loyal to Jesus Christ. Only then do we discover how wide is the mercy of God.

How narrow is narrow? No card playing? No movies? No "fun"? Is that it? Is that what it means to be narrow? We miss the whole point. How narrow is our loyalty to Jesus Christ? How narrow is our responsibility to love generously, give sacrificially, and accept others unconditionally? How narrow indeed.

The Far Gaze of God

*But while he was still far off, his father saw him
and was filled with compassion; he ran and put
his arms around him and kissed him.*
—Luke 15:20

Few would challenge the observation that the parable of the prodigal son is the most beloved parable our Lord taught. It is actually a parable about two sons and what at least one preacher has called "the prodigal father." Prodigal—often understood as deviant, reckless, wasteful—can also mean extravagant, lavish in giving, profuse. Prodigal. What we have here is a parable about a reckless, wasteful, younger son, an extravagant father, and a sullen, angry, bitter older son.

The father captures my imagination. Take a snapshot of that moment, a still photograph. "And while he was still far off, his father saw him." I'm thinking about the father's unbridled, extravagant, prodigal generosity. You know the story. The younger boy came to his dad one day and said, "Give me my portion." And the father did. As soon as the son received his inheritance, he left home. You can still hear the screen door slamming. Soon his life turned 180 degrees from the security, love, and safety of a home to reckless, wasteful living. The younger son became the wasteful son. He went to the far country. He lost himself in loose living.

We are told that a famine hit that land. Now we see a wasted son in a wasted place. This is a story of utter depravity. The boy was so hungry, so needy, that he did what no Jewish man or woman would do. He attached himself in absolute desperation to a swine farmer. He was sent out to feed pigs. He not only fed the pigs, but he looked like one. He smelled like one. There, in the pigsty, came the turning point in his life. The parable says, "He came to himself." He began to compose words, working on a "going-home" scenario. He said, "This is absolute insanity. This is the height of stupidity. How many of my father's hired men are eating three square meals a day and here I starve in this pigsty! I will arise and go to my father and will say, 'Father, I have sinned against heaven and against you.'" Do you see it? The father is always in focus in the story: "I will arise and go to my father." "I will say to my father . . . ."

He rehearsed the speech. He reconfigured his ego. He rediscovered homing instincts. He returned. William Augustus Jones rightly observed, "When the son turned for home, home turned to the son." Then, in the Scripture, these radical, wonderful words: "And while he was still a long way off, his father saw him and was filled with compassion."

The boy headed home. For his part, the father had been looking down that road for a long time. The father ran to his child. One commentator suggests the father probably lived in town. So the father had to throw propriety to the wind and run through the center of the village to escort his son through the gauntlet of under-breath sneers to come home. He ran to him. He threw his arms around him. More like a mother than a father, he kissed him. This is more than a Middle Eastern greeting. It is maternity in paternity—the tenderness of the father.

See the son standing before his father, held by great love. While in his father's embrace, the son began his speech. "Father, I've sinned against heaven and against you. I am no longer worthy to be called your son." But the father was not listening. He had already turned his head from the boy and shouted to the servants, "Quick! Bring the best robe and put it on him. Put a ring on his finger and sandals on his feet, kill the fattened calf, and let's have a party." The father swept up his son and escorted him through the middle of town. No telling what the people were thinking. Can you imagine the newspaper the next morning? All the while the boy was saying under his breath, "I can't believe this is my dad."

He took him to the house. They threw a big party. The music and the dancing were loud. Then we hear that dramatic, transitional word "meanwhile." The older son was in the field. He heard laughter. He heard music. He heard dancing. He heard noise. He heard party sounds from the house. He called a servant over and asked, "What is going on in there? I didn't order any party. I didn't schedule a dance band for this time of the day. What's going on in there?" "Oh, you haven't heard? Your brother has come home and your father has thrown a party for him."

Immediately, the older brother became sullen, withdrawn, taciturn, angry. The father went out to him. He listened to the older son's rebuke. The father in the story has me. He went out to his older boy. He listened. The older son unloaded all of his anger, his bitterness, his poison, his toxin. I am tempted to stop here and talk about that older son for just a moment, but I'm not going to do it. There is so much of him in all of us.

It is the father that has me. I want the father to have you. I want you to let the father walk into your soul for a moment. Don't you think God is like that? How far, how distant, how "out there" is the gaze of God? "While he was still a long way off, his father saw him." How far is the gaze of God? "While he was still far off . . . ."

There are some who don't believe God can see any further than the back pew of the church. Why? Because that is where they show up every Sunday for God to see them. Church is where God sees us best. You must be inside the four walls of the "God-box" for God to see you. God's vision, some say, is limited to the last pew. God looks there. God's gaze is fixed there. God sees me in church, so I'll be there. Maybe we think this way because in church, we most want to be seen. What do you think? How far is the gaze of God? How far can God see? How deep is God's look?

There are others who say, "God cannot see sin." I grew up hearing that theology. God cannot look on sin. This kind of reasoning believes that God turned God's back on the crucified Christ because God cannot see sin. Because Jesus took our sin upon himself and, in Paul's words, "became our sin," God cannot look on the crucified Jesus, hence our Lord's cry of God's forsakenness from the cross. That is how the argument goes.

One problem challenges this position, a problem exposed by the Bible. God can't see sin? Tell me, exactly what was God looking at when God saw Adam in the garden? God can't see sin? What was God looking at when God through Nathan looked at David and said, "You are the man"? God can't see sin? What about God in the presence of spies who visited with Rahab in Jericho? What do you think God saw that day? God can't see sin? What about Mary of Magadala and Peter of Capernaum? What about me? What about you? Here is an argument cobbled together with sheer nonsense.

God can't see sin? God is looking at sin all the time. God is looking at you and me. I ask again, how far is the gaze of God? "But while he was still a long way off, his father saw him and was filled with compassion and ran to him." It seems to me the far gaze of God is on the road. God's gaze is always a road look. God is a road warrior. God looks at the road. Tell me, how long do you think the father had been looking at the road? How many days do you think passed after the back door slammed and the younger son went out with his money to a far country? How long do you think it took before the dad started looking down that road for the son to come home? How long do you think the father looked at the only road that could bring his boy back?

God looks at the road. God knows what the road does to us. The road does something to all of us. The road of life puts blisters on our feet and takes us away from the house of God, from the love of God, from the embrace of God. It does something brutal to us. We leave with sandals; we come home without them. We leave with a robe; we come home naked. We leave with our stomachs filled; we come home with our stomachs empty. We leave home with rings on our fingers, and when we have pawned them all, we come home with empty fingers. God looks at the road. God doesn't look at sin? That is poppycock, baloney, and absurdity. God looks at the road. God is a road warrior whose gaze sees the road.

There is something more. God is not only looking at the road. God looks at the end of the road. The father wasn't looking at the sidewalk from the house to the street. He wasn't looking at the road that went down to the gate. No, the father was looking at the very end of the road, where the pavement met the horizon, where movement was first seen, the same place where you and I have the look and the feel and the smell of death itself. That is where God looks.

It is a lie that we have to get cleaned up or we have to be better before God will look at us. One of the sorrows of my soul in ministry is speaking and listening to people who unwind the saddest, most destructive of tales telling me of the brutality of life, what the road has done to them, what they have done on the road. Then to hear those words born of helplessness or seeming hopelessness, "Nobody could ever forgive me for what I've done." "No one would ever understand. No one." "If you knew me, you wouldn't love me."

"While he was far off, the father saw him." God not only looks at the road, but God sees the end of the road. When you and I feel as if we have come to the end of the road, when we have come to the end of all of our resources, my friend, look up. Turn your gaze 180 degrees because the Father's far gaze reaches the end of the road. God knows right where you are. "While he was far off, the father saw him."

But there is one more thing about this far gaze of God. God not only sees the road and the end of the road, but God sees you and me on the road. God is scanning the road. God's eyes are searching the point where the horizon meets the road. God's gaze always has an upward scan. God is looking at the end of the road, looking at the road's end for the smallest wiggle of movement. As soon as God sees movement at the end of the road, God's gaze moves up. Why? Because the Father is looking for you and for me on the road.

There is only one condition God gives for a reunion at home. We must take the first step toward the God who runs to us. We have to make a first step. We simply have to pirouette, simply turn toward home. If we take one step toward home, we discover the Father has made multiple steps at a full run toward us.

God's gaze not only looks at the road, but God is looking for us. God wants us to come home.

God throws caution to the wind. God is the reckless father who runs to us. See this reckless father, his robes flapping behind him. His arms are outstretched, tears spilling down his cheeks. He doesn't care what we look like or what we smell like or who we have hobnobbed with. He wants us home. He doesn't want to look down that road for us anymore. He wants us to come home.

Perhaps you enjoy, as I do, singing "Amazing Grace! How Sweet the Sound," penned by John Newton in the eighteenth century. It is the most beloved hymn among Christians around the world, "Amazing grace! How sweet the sound, that saved a wretch like me! I once was lost, but now am found, was blind, but now I see." John Newton wrote "Amazing Grace" at the age of fifty-four, but not until he had lived the life of a wretch. He was a trader in human flesh, a broker of slaves on the high seas. John Newton was an infidel of a man. He learned his trade from his father who was a seaman. His father taught him how to plow the high seas and showed him the money that could be made from trading humanity from one continent to another. Newton lived that life until God's "amazing grace" broke into his being.

Not only was he delivered from the slave ship in his past, but he was delivered to a pulpit. John Newton became a preacher. His whole life was changed. All Newton did was take one step toward God, who was always looking toward the end of the road for his lost son John Newton to come home.

John Newton died in 1807. He wrote his own epitaph. This is what it says: "John Newton, Clerk. Once an infidel and libertine, a servant of slaves in Africa: Was by the rich mercy of our Lord and Savior, Jesus Christ, Preserved, restored, pardoned, and appointed to preach the Faith he had labored so long to destroy."

Reading Newton's epitaph brings to mind the hauntingly joyful hymn with these words: "O the deep, deep love of Jesus, vast, unmeasured, boundless free! Rolling as a mighty ocean in its fullness over me, underneath me, all around me is current of Thy love leading onward, leading homeward, to my glorious rest above."

Here is the picture of God whose gaze reaches all the way to the end of the road, whose eyes gaze deeply into our own, whose arms reach out and bring us home. "While he was still far off, the father saw him."

Journey into Life

Desperate Measures

Jesus, Son of David, have mercy on me.
—Mark 10:47

In a 1933 edition of *The Atlantic Monthly*, Helen Keller published an essay that she titled "Three Days to See." This is what that great American woman said more than seventy years ago.

> I have often thought it would be a blessing if each human being were stricken blind and deaf for a few days at some time during his early adult life. Darkness would make him more appreciative of sight; silence would teach him the joys of sound.
>
> Now and then I have tested my seeing friends to discover what they see. Recently I was visited by a very good friend who had just returned from a long walk in the woods, and I asked her what she had observed. "Nothing in particular," she replied. I might have been incredulous had I not been accustomed to such responses, for long ago I became convinced that the seeing see little.[1]

At times, the seeing are blind. The prophet Isaiah, speaking to God's people in the sixth century BC, said much the same thing: "Therefore, justice is far from us, and righteousness does not reach us; we wait for light, and lo! there is darkness; and for brightness, but we walk in gloom" (Isa 59:9). But I suspect few of us identify with the prophet's analysis of life. I would suspect that more than a few of us are not in the realm of gloom. Perhaps gloom is the least likely word to describe your life.

Maybe the word delight is a better word. Delight. What a wonderful word. The psalmist said, "I delight to do your will, O my God. Your law is within my heart" (Ps 40:8). Delight describes the heart's joy unlike any word in our vocabulary. She is older now. But a few years ago, I sat on the platform steps of the sanctuary of the First Baptist Church of Augusta before the first morning service with three-year-old Victoria. She was waiting for her mother to finish practicing the hand bells so she could go to extended session and Sunday School. As I looked into her eyes, I saw delight in every glimmer, in every dimple on her flawless face.

How true it is for all of us from time to time. When the word delight clothes us in its wonder, we linger in a timeless place. Do you remember when your daughter took her first steps? Do you remember when your son said his first words? Do you remember when your child walked across a stage and received a diploma? Do you remember when you walked into your first home? I remember. But delight, like happiness, like laughter, like tears, does not last long. We delight in brief glimpses, sunburst smiles, a tender touch. There are delightful moments but few delightful days.

And yes, the witness of the Bible reveals another side of delight. We can too easily delight in that which is not good. Later in Isaiah, the prophet spoke of God's people with these harsh words: "[They] have chosen their own ways, and in their abominations they take delight" (Isa 66:3). To our sorrow, we who are made in God's image can and do delight even in behaviors that diminish our humanity and mar our glory. Regardless, in joy or shame, delight lasts for only a moment. And when delight passes, life returns to whatever is "normal," with memories of more joyous moments clouded by either life's demands or worse, dark disillusionment.

How many could you number among your friends who have known the delights of life only to be pummeled into the cavernous gully of disillusionment? How many have you known who in one moment were pirouetting on the dance floor of life to wonderful music and the next found themselves shoved into the grip of a brutal, terrible disappointment? Fellow church members who once knew great joy in serving Christ are now numbered among the cynically disillusioned. Parents who once knew delight with their children now wake up into a nightmare of rebellion, anger, and failure, disillusioned.

There is short, touchable distance between delight and disillusionment. The Bible knows this reality all too well. Look at David the king, dancing before the ark. Then see him in a few flickers of time quaking before his own son Absalom as rebellion stirs itself in the kingdom. Look at Peter boasting about his loyalty to Jesus, only to slink out of town with denial on his lips and disillusionment in his soul. Delight often and quickly moves to disillusionment. Disillusionment, left unchecked, can move to despair.

His name is Bartimaeus. The first time we meet him, he is on the ground: he is hugging earth, covered with dust, plying his trade, whiling away the hours of life no doubt in a kind of cynical despair. We are told he is there on the fast track of life known in those parts as the Jericho road. There he sits, begging. There was no more highly trafficked road during the time of Jesus than the Jericho road. The Jericho road was like I-75 into Atlanta; it was the main highway. Anybody who was somebody came by that way as they journeyed up and down the Jerusalem highway. You passed through or by Jericho as you traveled to David's city, the superhighway to Jerusalem. Everybody went through Jericho to get to Jerusalem. Modern day travelers still do.

There he was, beside the road, sitting in a beggar's goldmine. Yet Bartimaeus was marginalized; he was beside the main road. In a word, he was a roadside entrepreneur. His vocation was asking, begging for anything anybody would give him.

Bartimaeus was as about as low on the human ladder as you could get. See the despair etched on this man's weathered face. Mind you, he has not been there an hour, or a few hours in the morning. He has not been there a day, weeks, or even months. He has been there most of his life. How many of us, regardless of how we are dressed, regardless of what our financial statement says, regardless of what people say about us, could say, "That's me. That's where I am. I see life moving by. I see people moving on with life, and yet I'm trapped, breathing dust along a Jericho road." Delight can move to disillusionment and disillusionment often moves to despair.

But Bartimaeus had something going for him that he didn't know he had going for him. A wonderful gift was coming his way. Jesus was on that road. Just a question: Why is it that we would choose death when life is passing by? Why would anybody who knew that life and light, sight and joy was walking by stay begging by the road? Why would anybody do that? I don't know, but many do.

There he was. But somehow, he had heard the word. No doubt he had heard the name "Jesus"—Jeshua in Hebrew. Jeshua, Joshua, Jesus in English. Jeshua meant "Deliverer." That's the word he longed to hear—Jesus. So he began shouting like a madman, "Jesus, Son of David, have mercy on me."

Mind you, Jesus is there, but so are other travelers. Notice the people traveling with Jesus on the road—the people who were mobile, the people who were seeing, the people who were occupying the road. Immediately, they turned to this guy and said, "Why don't you shut up? Be quiet! You are an embarrassment." But he is numb to the crass put-down. Bartimaeus had heard and felt it all. "You are a nobody, you will always be a nobody. Just be quiet, lest the famous teacher get the wrong impression of Jericho."

Bartimaeus was desperate. I wonder if you are. Am I? He cried out again, "Jesus, Son of David, have mercy on me!" Jesus heard the voice, heard the name, and felt the cry. And he stopped. In fact, in the Greek language, the verb used here suggests that Jesus had already stopped. Jesus stopped after the first cry. He turned to the crowd and said, "Call that man. Bring him to me." So we are told Bartimaeus threw off his cloak, rose, and felt his way to Jesus. He stumbled his way to Jesus and then stood in the presence of all presences. Jesus asked him the same question Jesus is asking us. "What do you want me to do for you?"

If you read the entire tenth chapter of Mark, you will find this same question. Just prior to Jesus' encounter with Bartimaeus, James and John, those "sons of thunder," come to Jesus and say, "Teacher, we want you to do for us whatever we ask" (Mark 10:35-45). Do you remember Jesus' response? "What do you want me to do for you?" And they said, "Grant one to sit on the right and one on the left when you enter your kingdom." In other words, "We would like you to elevate us to a place of prominence. That's what we would like."

Don't miss it. The request of those disciples is so far from Bartimaeus's need. Bartimaeus doesn't need power; he needs sight and light and life. He is not looking for a place at a banquet. He is looking for a simple place in life. He is looking for a little light—a little sight.

I wonder how many of us act more like James and John and yet know deep inside that our name is Bartimaeus. How many of us have spent more than a little bit of our lives trying to find the limelight at the right or the left? I wonder how many of us would say, "I've spent years, decades, trying to get in that place of prominence—left side, right side, that higher place on the ladder. And now, after years of craving position, I've discovered it's an empty quest." Now, at mid-life, at mid-career, at mid-marriage, at mid-whatever, you know that you are Bartimaeus. You realize you have been on the dusty road all the time and didn't know it. Now Jesus says, "What do you want me to do for you?"

"If I could just have sight. If I could see my wife, the dimples in my children's face, a sunset, a running spring. I've known gloom too long. All I want to do is see." Jesus looked at Bartimaeus and said, "Go. Your faith has already made you well." In fact, the word in the original language is the word we often translate "saved." "Your faith has saved you [made you whole]." Mark tells us that immediately, sight came to those blind eyes. In that moment when he saw, the last phrase of the tenth verse says that "he followed him on the way." Bartimaeus joined up with Jesus and followed him.

I wonder if delight has been lost somewhere in your soul, so much so that all you know now is disillusionment, even despair. In spite of everything everybody else thinks about you, you know in your soul that there is a desperate person living inside your skin. The road is so dusty and the sun so hot and the day so long and the darkness so deep that you would give anything to see.

Jesus is passing by. Jesus is listening. How many could say, "I've been blinded by the brokenness of life"? We human beings are slow at this. We don't learn this quickly; in fact, some never learn it at all. Learn what? That life has a broken dimension that we cannot escape. Your health is going to fail one day and you can't escape that. The people you love most are going to disappoint you and you can't escape that. In fact, you are going to disappoint them probably more than they are going to disappoint you. There is a broken side to the human experience that none of us can fix. Like so many, you may be blinded by the fact, the inescapable reality of human brokenness. You are in a dark place because you think God is cruel or life is hard and ought not to be that way. Listen to the story: at times, life is brutally that way. The sooner we make peace with it, the sooner we throw off the rags of prominence and pride, the sooner we take desperate measures crying out for Jesus, the sooner we are going to see.

Where some struggle with the brutality of life, others are blinded by theological or spiritual darkness. You can't quite make sense of the Bible. You wrestle with all kinds of theological difficulties. There are philosophical blind spots. You can't quite figure it all out. Truth to tell, there is an obtuse dimension to our relationship with God. None of us are ever going to figure it all out. Even Jesus hung on a splintered cross and asked, "My God, my God, why have you forsaken me?" He didn't figure it all out. He simply trusted. But what do we do? We spend a great deal of our time and no small amount of energy trying to find "the theological key." If you find it, go and take God's place. Some people are blinded by theological darkness. They think there ought to be some system, some way that makes sense of faith, doubt, God, life, you name it.

Then more than a few of us are simply blinded by the dust fellow travelers kick up along the way. We are in the human experience, and what's happening in other people's lives kicks up dust in our faces. This dust from other travelers makes us uncomfortable with life because we can't make peace with the fact that people are the way they are.

I've heard it throughout my ministry. In fact, I heard it before I got in the ministry: some Christian people say they quit being a part of the Christian community because somebody hurt their feelings. Somebody let them down. It could have been a preacher, a deacon, a Sunday School teacher. Road dust thrown in your face is going to happen. It is part of the human package. Mind you, I'm not excusing it. I'm simply saying that the dust people kick up is going to land on you from time to time. If you are not careful, it will blind you.

But Jesus is walking by. In your desperation, you can cry out to Jesus. The good news is that Jesus has already stopped. He has already stopped in order to listen and respond to you. He is saying right now wherever you are, "Get up, come to me." When you come to Jesus in your desperation he will give you sight. And when he does, get busy following Jesus on the way, that superhighway that is the Way, the Truth, and the Life. Jesus will put you back in life when you follow him.

In all candor, when you are desperate, the last thing you need is to figure it out. What you need is someone you can follow who can give you sight. Bartimaeus learned that. So can we. Yes, when you follow Jesus, you are in Jesus' company. In Jesus' company, you start seeing life through the eyes of Jesus. When you see life through the eyes of Jesus, you will end up at a Calvary someplace, and you will give your life for somebody or something somewhere that may take a death in order to find life.

In all candor, when you follow Jesus on the road, you will discover that grabbing everything you can grab and accumulating the most toys before you die is neither the goal of life nor life's purpose. You will discover that in spite of human brokenness and theological ambiguity, human sin and disappointment, that when you follow Jesus you always see what matters most.

"I've been astonished," wrote Helen Keller, that in my life of observation, "the seeing see little." What about you? Delight? Disillusionment? Despair? Get up out of the dust. Come to Jesus. Receive his gift of sight, and get busy following him.

[1] Helen Keller, as quoted in *The Atlantic Monthly* (November 1997).

From Death to Life

Very truly, I tell you, anyone who hears my word and believes him who sent me has eternal life, and does not come under judgment, but has passed from death to life.
—John 5:24

She sits in a room alone. It's toward the end of the day. There is no need to draw the shades. All of the inner lights of her life have gone down. She is going through the valley of the shadow of grief. There is a weeping soul in the cavernous quiet of her life. And yet, the still, small voice of Jesus keeps whispering over and over, "I am the resurrection and the life."

He has come to mid-life with some measure of professional success. Still, there is within him a hunger no promotion satisfies, no accomplishment fills. He is hungry for something more. In a word, he is famished spiritually. He would give up but for the words of Jesus: "I am the bread of life."

Life. Jesus spoke so often of life. You could say his whole message was life. "I have come that they may have life." "I am the light of life." "For God so loved the world that he gave his only son that whosoever believes in him should not perish, but have everlasting life." Life was what Jesus was all about. Jesus was and is the embodiment of life. Jesus is God's "life gift" to us and within us.

One day, our Lord was in the city of Jerusalem attending a feast. There, on the north side of the temple area, was a pool of water. You can still see it today. It is the Pool of Bethesda. Around this pool were five porticos. It was a place where people came and went, perhaps hundreds, maybe thousands, but they were always the regular residents: the sick, the lame, the diseased.

Legend said that in this pool, an occasional zephyr of wind would ripple the water. It was believed that the rippling of the water was the flutter of angel wings.

If you could get in the pool at the time of the rippling of the water, you would receive a miraculous cure for your illness. Who wouldn't show up for that?

All around this pool were sick folks holding on to phantom hope. Call it magic, maybe superstition, but many waited for cures that never came. Don't we do the same thing? Don't we have our unfounded superstitions about how God works and the way God works? How many times have I had private conversations with Christians—I'm talking Bible-believing people, Sunday School members with ten-year attendance pins—who ask, "Preacher, doesn't the Bible say . . . ?" I listen politely and reply, "My friend, that is fascinating wisdom, but that is not in the Bible. Maybe Ben Franklin said it, or popular legend, but that is not the Bible." We too have our pools of water. We too wait with hollow expectation; maybe angels will flutter waters, maybe something will happen that will give me what I deeply, desperately need. But nothing happens. No one shows up.

A lame man was there. The Bible says he had hung around that pool for thirty-eight years. Understand this as a lifetime. He had been there most of his life waiting for the moment when the waters would ripple so he could get in and be healed. Jesus came along, saw him there, and said, "My friend, do you want to be well?" Do I, do we want to be well? The man said what we say in moments like this. "Well, Lord, I would like to be well, but you know how it is here. There are so many people around this pool; the waters ripple, everybody gets in before me, and I never have a chance."

"Get up! Stand up! Don't give me your excuses. Stand up!" Jesus lifted the man to his feet. Look at him. I imagine he not only walked; I imagine he skipped. He probably ran from that place. You don't need rippling water when Life tells you to get up. Now all would have been well except for a calendar problem. It was not an ordinary day. It was the Sabbath. The Sabbath is for reading the Bible. The Sabbath is for going to the synagogue. The Sabbath is for doing holy things. You don't heal people on the Sabbath. So a controversy ensued. Jesus was right in the middle of it. Our Lord's opponents said, "Healing is work. You shouldn't work." It is out of that controversy that we read these awesome words: "I tell you the truth, whoever hears my word and believes him who sent me has eternal life and will not be condemned; he has crossed over from death to life."

Death may be *the* contemporary obscenity. Yet we have a curious fascination with life's terminal reality. Have you ever thought about it? We have an almost sick relationship with death. We only whisper "death" in polite conversation. But then we pay $7 a ticket to see it on the big screen and call it entertainment. I'm told that before a child reaches his or her maturity, he or she will witness tens of thousands of murders on the television screen and in the movie theater. Tell me, is that not sick? Shh. Death.

Our culture's take on death is such that we deny it. We see it as failure, even defeat. Some say, "Death is sin." As you might imagine, the Bible has a different take on death. The Bible says death is not so much something that happens to us. Rather, death is an integral part of who we are. Death is not something external to our human experience. Death is within the human experience. It is part of being a *homo sapien*, a human being.

A few years ago, a scary movie hit the theaters. When I talk about films in sermons, I am not endorsing them. Please don't write me a letter. I do believe that films today are expressing our culture; they are telling us something about our collective consciousness, who we are as people. I think Christian people are wise to watch films critically and ask, "What is this movie saying to the larger culture about God, life, theology?"

The movie was *The Sixth Sense*. It starred Bruce Willis and a cute little boy named Haley Joel Osment. Osment's character has, according to the script, a unique gift. He is afraid to tell anybody about this gift, so he whispers, "I see dead people . . . walking around like real people." The film moves with that idea.

Truth to tell, the movie is only half wrong. The Bible says, "All of us are seeing dead people walking around." Until we have a relationship with God in Jesus Christ, every one of us is dead (Eph 2:1-2). We may look alive. We may breathe. We may eat and drink and sleep and do all the things living people do. We may marry and have children and have all the outward signs of being alive. But until we have a relationship with God through Jesus Christ, the Scripture says we are dead, D-E-A-D. "I see dead people. I see dead people walking around."

There is no escaping death. It is the inescapable fact of our existence. The same Bible that says we are dead without a spiritual birth in Christ goes on to say there is the possibility of being freed from the power of death. We do not meet death at the end of life. My friend, we are in death now. We are in death until a greater reality, an amazing grace, comes over us in Christ that frees us from death's grip, fear, and power.

Did you hear Jesus? "Whoever hears my words and believes him who sent me has eternal life now. He has crossed over from death to life." The man at the pool had been there for thirty-eight years. He looked alive. He was crippled. He could not walk. He was confined to a pallet. There were signs that his life was not full. But notice: he was living and breathing, seeing and eating and sleeping. He looked alive, but there was the reality of death in him as it is in all of us until Jesus comes our way and says, "Stand up!"

The human experience, however, tells us we can die without dying. The Bible says we can be dead without dying. Martin Luther King Jr., who gave us so many eloquent truths about life, said as much a long time ago. "The way to kill a bird is not to shoot it," said King. "The way to kill a bird is to clip its wings. For when you clip a bird's wings you kill its 'bird-itis'; you destroy what makes it a bird."[1] We all know that a person can die without dying. Some of us are clawing our way through the morgue right now.

So many are dead without dying: lost hope, terminal despair, pathological cynicism, immobilizing fear. Hear the Bible at two levels. Physical death is inescapable. Spiritual death is optional. Every one of us decides on the option of spiritual death. Both of these realities meet us every day. We are living life at two levels, aware that our physical bodies will one day give up the ghost, someone will call the mortician, and we will be cremated or buried. But the spiritual reality is that we can be walking around and yet be dead on the inside.

When we face that fact, we have two options. The first option is to be terrorized by our own death and our dying, our emptiness inside. We can choose to be terrorized with fear, anger, bitterness, cynicism, and so forth. Or we can trust another who can help us cross over from the terror of death into life.

How do we choose trust over terror? How do we move from death to life? The answer is profoundly simple. First, we accept a gift. The man at the pool that day could have said to Jesus, "I'm not getting up. I've been here thirty-eight years. I know these people. It's bad, but I'm here. Go heal somebody else." But instead the man accepted the gift Jesus gave him. When Jesus said, "Stand up," the man stood up. How do we move from death to life? We accept a gift.

Paul was on to this idea in Ephesians 2:3-10. He told the Ephesians (my paraphrase), "All of you were dead in your trespasses and sins. But God made you alive through Christ. For by grace are you saved through faith. It is not that of yourselves, it is the gift of God." How do we move from death to life? First, we realize that the gift we need is not something we create. By definition as human beings, we are dead. Only the gift of God can give life. First, we accept a gift.

How do you move from death to life? Celebrate life: your life, another's life, God's life. Life. We celebrate the life God gives us, a life of grace and love. We celebrate the people in our lives who make life rich. How do you move from death to life? Celebrate life.

I do not understand and have never understood cynical, negative, bitter Christians. Like you, I get there every once in a while myself, but I never like myself when I get there. My preacher back home called it the "mully-grubs." Some people strangely seem to enjoy the mully-grubs. So much about these poor folks is saying, "Yeah, I'm going to heaven, but this life is terminally terrible."

They are negative, cynical, backbiting. I know some people who try to be positive, but they are really negative. How is that? They have little side conversations going on that are put-downs of others.

At a church banquet years ago, Dr. Thomas Blanchard, a now-deceased gifted urologist and giant churchman, reminded the attendees at an after-dinner talk how Southerners negotiate the subtle put-down. Tommy deftly used humor to remind us all how we demolish another person by simply adding the words, "Bless her heart." "She's ugly, bless her heart." Or, "Bless his heart, he can't stop cheating on his wife." I could give other examples, but you know how the put-down works. In any disguise, negative, cynical, cutting language and attitudes deal in death.

Is there a way out of this malicious matrix, this death-dealing reality in which we find ourselves as human beings? How do you move from death to life? For starters, we can celebrate life. Jesus Christ came to make life abundant with a capital L. Anytime we of faith accept a gift, that gift puts the responsibility on us to celebrate the life that is in that gift, the very life of Christ within.

How do we move from death to life? We trust the Savior. We place our trust in Jesus Christ. Our money says, "In God we trust," but none of us believe it. We talk about trusting this person and that person or that idea or this group of people. Every four years, we are asked to trust a handful of presidential and congressional candidates. Like you, I've been there and done that. How do we move from death to life? We put our trust in Jesus Christ.

The old hymns say it best. "My hope is built on nothing less than Jesus blood and righteousness." "Trusting Jesus every day, trusting through a stormy way; even when my faith is small, trusting Jesus, that is all." I'm convinced that people live under the burden and the pain of death. I do, you do, we do when we move from trust to terror. My friend, death will stalk you; invite the living Christ to be your life. Trust the Savior.

How do we move from death to life? We give ourselves back to others. This may be the most important step of all. How do you move from death to life? Give yourself back to others. I don't know what has happened in the American church today, but we have an awful case of Christian narcissism. "I'm going to heaven. I'm saved." A few years ago a bumper sticker made its way around the country that said, "I found it." The unsaid message was, "Sorry about you."

I am saved by the grace of God, I believe eternal life is God's gift to me in grace, and I am a Christian. But the Christian faith is not primarily "me" or "you" focused. The Christian faith says, "I have received a gift, I celebrate life, I trust the Savior," all for the purpose of giving back to others. I have found in life, and particularly in church life, that the negative, cynical, angry people, whether within or without the church—but particularly within the church—are folks who have simply turned all the lights in the world on themselves. My kids say to me sometimes when I get self-absorbed, "Dad, get a life." What they are saying is, "Give your life back to someone; turn your life inside out by giving to others." Isn't that what God calls us to do?

For some reason, we thought early on that our life was supposed to be a big cup to fill with all the goodness of God. And when the cup became full, we were going to enjoy it ourselves. The Scriptures give us another picture. Before coming to Christ, we are an opaque, dull, cold lump of stone. When we come to faith in Christ, he turns our dull, dense lives into a brilliant mirror from which the light and the life of God are reflected back on other people.

"I see dead people. I see dead people walking around." Are you dead or are you alive? Physical death is inescapable. Spiritual death is optional. Which will you choose?

[1] This quote from Martin Luther King, Jr. came from a conversation I had several years ago with William Augustus Jones, Jr., who heard Dr. King make this statement a number of times.

Upside Down

In the temple he found people selling cattle, sheep, and doves, and the money changers seated at their tables.
—*John 2:14*

The question with which we wrestle during the season of Lent is a question that has survived all the centuries of the Christian church. "Who is Jesus?" Albert Schweitzer, the Nobel Prize winning humanitarian, who was also an organist, a physician, and a theologian, wrote in 1906 a work titled in English *The Quest for the Historical Jesus*. It was a magisterial, scholarly work in which Schweitzer traced all of the various lives of Jesus that had been written in the nineteenth century. It was quite fashionable at that time to write a life of Jesus. The French scholar Ernest Renan wrote of the romantic Jesus. The Germans wrote of the rational Jesus, and so forth. Schweitzer went back and looked at all of those lives of Jesus and then shared his own understanding of Jesus' life and ministry.

One of the last lines of his work is both memorable and haunting: "He comes to us as one unknown, without a name." Who is Jesus? I pick up the Gospels and wonder, as many times as I have read the stories of Jesus' life, if I really know who he is. I wonder if you do. I wonder if we do. During Lent, we force the question, all the while following this One who goes before us to a lonely cross and a silent grave.

Who Is Jesus? The writer of the Fourth Gospel shows us by telling a story recorded in John 2:13-25 through which Jesus is revealed as the upside-down Messiah. Our Lord is the one who inverts reality. Jesus does 180-degree pirouettes on nearly every definition of life that we think is nailed down. Jesus turns things upside down.

The story takes place in the Jerusalem Temple during the time of our Lord's life. The year is probably AD 26. In 20 BC, Herod the Great began to rebuild the Jerusalem Temple, and what an incredible building project it was. When you go to Israel today, you see evidence of the building projects of Herod the Great almost everywhere you travel. In his brief reign, he did more building than perhaps any other ruler in that part of the world at any other time. He began rebuilding the temple in 20 BC. That project continued after his death and was not complete until AD 64. It was a building project that spanned eighty-four years.

Words that describe the Temple Herod built in Jerusalem are *magnificent, opulent, extravagant, overwhelming.* In fact, so overwhelming was the Temple in its architectural wonder and beauty that the disciples, as recorded by Mark during the last days of our Lord's life, looked at the Temple and exclaimed, "What magnificent buildings" (Mark 13:1). Anyone who came near Jerusalem could see the Temple glistening in the Middle Eastern sun. The Temple was like a brilliant diamond.

Remember this about the Temple. The economy of Jerusalem was the Temple and the Temple was the Jerusalem economy. All subsidiary industries, all other entrepreneurial ventures, all merchant endeavors, all manufacturing of anything, all of it tied in to the economy of Jerusalem through the conduit of the Temple. Had the Temple not been in Jerusalem, there would have been no reason for the city to be there. The Temple was the reason for Jerusalem's existence.

We are told in this text that it is Passover time (John 2:13-22). Every male within fifteen miles of the city was required under Jewish Law to celebrate Passover in Jerusalem. Pilgrims would come from all over the ancient world for their pilgrimage to Jerusalem, there to celebrate the Passover in the Holy City. And therein is the problem.

The purpose of the Temple was worship. But the business of the Temple was ritual. The Temple's purpose could not be carried out without the business of the Temple going on. In order for the Temple to be effective and useful, the business of the ritual around the Temple had to take place. The Temple economy, the Temple ritual, the Temple worship, and visitors to the city all tied in with each other. In fact, Jews were required to spend their tithes in the city of Jerusalem. As the money flowed, the city flourished.

The business cycle worked like this: Worship required sacrifice, and sacrifice required approved, perfect, certified animals. Worshipers purchased those perfect certified animals with money, and that money could only be Temple money that was exchanged in the Temple from the Temple treasury. The Temple business had the Temple worship and the Jerusalem economy locked up. Why? Because one couldn't sacrifice just any animal. A worshiper had to sacrifice an "approved animal," bought from approved people who were tied in to the Temple economy.

Money used to purchase those animals was Temple currency. So if you brought your coins from Rome or Egypt or wherever, that currency had to be changed in the Temple so that you could purchase an approved, certified animal for sacrifice. All of the economy was wrapped up in the worship and business of the Temple. In this opulent, magnificent, awesome place, worship was held hostage to business.

Christians have used the story before us through the years to tell us that nothing can be bought or sold in the church house. I know what you are thinking; you are going where I've been. You have been taught as have I that this text tells us that no changing of money is to take place in the church house. There are to be no bake sales, no book sales, no exchanging of money of any kind; that's off limits in the church house because the Bible says you are not suppose to sell cookies in the church. That is what we have all grown up with. That's what this text means, doesn't it?

I remember well the second church we served in Kentucky. The women of the church decided they wanted to have a bazaar. More than a few men of the church thought that was bizarre. Let me tell you something, guys. If the women of the church want to do something, don't fight it. Bless it. So the women of Hillcrest Baptist Church, Frankfort, Kentucky, decided to have a bazaar for the purpose of raising money for missions. This conversation about whether or not we were going to have the bazaar went on for a long time. In the halls, in the Sunday School classrooms. Are we going to do this or not do this? Do you know what? No one was listening to our text. We thought Jesus' cleansing of the Temple had something to do with cookie sales. And we still do.

I suggest there is another problem in this text. There is something else in this story that is far more troubling than whether we are going to have a bazaar at the church. It is this "something else" that has me. I want you to think about two words that walk out of this story into our lives. The first is the word *barriers*. This story tells us that Jesus turns upside down every barrier to God in our lives. You know and I know and God knows that we have a host of them. Let me mention four.

One of the barriers we have in our lives that keep us from God and from others is conventional wisdom. How many of us live with sentences beginning, "I have always believed . . ."? We call that conventional wisdom. Conventional wisdom is that which is handed down from generation to generation, often uncritically. It is simply what we have always been told. Whether it is so or not so, whether it squares with our experience of God in Christ and our understanding of who God is in our day and in our time is absolutely superfluous. "I've always been told."

You have heard the story about the new bride who decided to host all of her family members for a big dinner. She told her husband to go out and buy a whole ham. He did. He went and bought the whole ham and no sooner had he brought it home than she said, "Bring me a saw." He said, "For what?" She said, "I've got to cut this ham in two." So he went out to the garage and brought a saw to his bride. She cut the ham in two, putting the shank in the freezer and the nice meaty portion in a pan for baking. He said, "Why did you do that?" She said, "That's how my mother cooked a ham." He said, "That's crazy. Why didn't you fix the whole thing?" "No," she said, "that's how we do it."

On the day of the gathering, everybody showed up at the house, and the baked ham was placed on the table. The new groom took his mother-in-law aside and said, "Tell me something. I went out and bought a ham for your daughter. She sawed it in half and baked the meaty part and put the other half into the freezer. Why did she do that?" Her mother said, "That's what my mom always taught us to do." He said, "Really?" She said, "That's what mom always did."

The grandmother was at the party. So he went to her with the same question. "You know your granddaughter told me to go out a buy a ham." He told her the whole story. "Why does she do that? Your daughter says that's the way you always prepared it." The grandmother smiled real big and said, "Well, to be honest with you, when I was taking up housekeeping with her granddaddy, we didn't have no pan big enough to put the whole ham in."

Here is the dark side of conventional wisdom. Conventional wisdom can be a barrier between God and us. Why was this changing of money going on in the Temple? Because it always had. No one had the courage or conviction to challenge the conventional wisdom that ran the Temple business.

A second barrier in our lives may be theological systems. God knows we have more of them than we can kill. Calvinism, Augustinianism, Thomism, Fundamentalism, Liberalism—all theological systems crafted by human minds and passed on from generation to generation. All of us are products of all of those theological systems and more. For the most part, every one of them is more fascinating to study than it is applicable to contemporary life.

If you were to line up John Calvin, John Wesley, St. Augustine, the leaders of the fundamentalist movement, the leading voices within contemporary liberalism, and every other theological "ism" in Christendom, you would discover one common trait. Every one of them exists, then or now, for the purpose of helping people get in touch with God. The purpose of any theological model is to enable, empower, engage one's relationship with God. The goal is God, not the system. If your theological system is so important that you have to sever relationships with people over what you believe theologically, you have probably lost touch with God.

Barriers. The first century Jewish leaders had a theological system in the Temple to beat the band. It was set up to a great degree to exclude people from God rather than to include people in a relationship with God.

A third barrier is often sociological categories. Do you live on this side of town or "the other" side of town? Do you come from money or from poverty? Are you educated or uneducated? What clubs include you as a member, and how are you connected in the community? If your connections are all that important in the community, stop and ask yourself from time to time whether your connections are enabling you to tell people about God in Jesus Christ or whether they are just an ego trip for you to feel good about yourself.

There is not one tie we have with others in our community—business, money, education, leadership—that is not a gift from God to enable us to connect our lives to people with the message of Christ. All our social connections are gifts from God, avenues to share the love of God with others.

Remember the story in the first chapter of John, where Phillip said he had found the Messiah (John 1:35-51)? Philip said to his buddy Nathaniel, "Nathaniel, we found the Messiah." "Who's that?" "Jesus of Nazareth." Nathaniel grumbled and said, "Nazareth? Can any good thing come out of Nazareth?" "Oh, not much, Nathaniel. Just the Son of God." Why was Nathaniel so prejudiced? In that day, Nazareth was the slum district of Galilee. Sociological categories all too easily breed racism, class-ism, gender-ism, and exclusive-ism. All of them together breed a noxious snobbery that is offensive to God and contrary to the message and meaning of the gospel. Barriers.

One more: political loyalty. In our country, we have at least every four years an exciting, frustrating, at times confusing political debate. Lest you think it doesn't get any worse than we have it now, think again. Times have been worse and, yes, times have been better. The truth is, this is our time. We would be wise to be careful as believers in Jesus Christ that we don't confuse our political alliances with the kingdom of God. Whether you are a Democrat, a Republican, an Independent, or whatever, don't ever become so linked with your politics that you think your particular political persuasion is the answer to all of humanity's problems. Every political system is fatally flawed because its foundation is human sinfulness and people. Barriers. Jesus Christ came to reveal to us the kingdom of God and to show us how the kingdom of God can break into our lives with its power, its love, and its grace.

Henri Nouwen died all too soon. His death is still sending shock waves across the Christian family. We miss him. He penned a few lines that cast light on our subject. "The real enemies of our life are the 'Oughts' and the 'Ifs,'" wrote Nouwen. "They pull us backward into the unalterable past and forward into the unpredictable future. But real life places us in the here and now. God is a God of the present." When we meet Jesus, we meet someone who is revealing God to us here and now. Get hooked up with God here, now. And if your sociology, theology, political science, conventional wisdom, racism, genderism, or whatever is keeping you from God, throw it down, turn it over, get rid of it. No human-made barrier is worth your life. In Jesus' presence, we must ask, "Do I know God?"

Who is Jesus? He is the one who breaks down barriers.

The second word is *security*. Jesus not only breaks down the barriers that keep us from God, but Jesus overturns all human-made security with resurrection life. Long ago, when you stood in the shadow of the Temple, you stood in the shadow of a structure, an architectural wonder that would give anyone some sense of physical security. It was awesome. But Jesus said, "Destroy this Temple, and in three days I will raise it." They said, "That's ridiculous. It's taken forty-six years to get us this far. But he was speaking not of the outward structure of the Temple. He was speaking of the spiritual reality where God's presence dwelt, the Temple of his body. He was talking about the Temple of his life pointing to his resurrection.

Jesus is the upside-down prophet because he not only attacks the barriers in our lives that stand between us and God and others. He also comes to tell us that there is only one source of security against which we can lean our lives. That immovable source of security is not our physical health or our material wealth; it's not even standing in the shadow of a great cathedral. That ultimate security comes only from God.

Through the years, I have had the privilege of leading churches to build or renovate buildings for ministry. My present ministry with Resource Services, Inc. (RSI) allows me the joy of working with churches to raise needed capital to buy property, relocate, or expand ministry by building new facilities. In my judgment, there is only one reason for churches to own property and erect buildings: to offer space in which and through which people can connect with God and others. Churches are people places where people gather to experience the love of God and the reality of the fellowship of the church. The church is to be a place where barriers are broken down, where class and race and color and language and social standing mean absolutely nothing. When we walk through church doors, we become either brother or sister. God knows we all need someplace on this planet where we are simply accepted for who we are.

What are the barriers in your life that are keeping you from God and from others? Have you built such a neat and tidy system around you that God can't even break through your system to love you, bless you, and free you? Are you walking around tighter than a three-dollar watch instead of free as a son or daughter of God? What are the barriers? And where is your security? Is it in your health, your social status, your connectedness, your money? Or is it in God?

Who is Jesus? Jesus is the One who tells us that every one of us is in need of a Savior. He turned reality upside down. He broke down every barrier for one godly reason: to love us back to the God who made us. Why don't you let him do that for you? Why don't you let God do for you what you cannot do for yourself? If you will, you will see the barriers fall down. When they do, you will discover an inner security that will square the shoulders of your soul and help you look up into the light of the face of God.

¹ As cited in *Context*, ed. Martin Marty (February 1997).

The Sacrament of Suffering

Then he began to teach them that the Son of Man must undergo great suffering.
—Mark 8:31

Suffering colors with dark tones every utterance of our Lord in the season of Lent. "Man of sorrows! What a name for the Son of God who came." He is the man of sorrows. He is acquainted with grief. He is the One who goes before us in suffering love and death to show us that the way of sacrifice, the way of death, the way of self-giving is indeed the way of love and the way of life. Mark 8:31-38 is the record of the first of three predictions our Lord made regarding his suffering and death in Jerusalem. Prior to the details of that awful moment in Jerusalem when Jesus dies on the cross, we find these words: "The Son of Man must undergo great suffering, and be rejected, and be killed, and rise again on the third day."

Like you, I've read this text any number of times. For the first time, as I looked at the text recently, I noticed there may be a created distance by the first tiny comma in Jesus' words. "The Son of Man must undergo great suffering, and be rejected, and be killed, and rise again the third day." His suffering seems almost separate from his dying. Though in fact our Lord's suffering and dying are not separate, he may be saying to all of us that suffering is found not only in dying; rather, suffering is a living thing, a part of our existence not always associated with the end of human life.

Examples abound. I think of two from the Bible. Think of that moment in the Old Testament when the aged patriarch Abraham hears God say, "Abraham, take your son, your only son Isaac, to the mountain I will show you, and there, sacrifice him as an offering to me." At that moment, when Abraham said "Yes" to God, the dagger of suffering was thrust into his soul. Why? Because he was being obedient to God, knowing if he carried out that command, not only would he kill his only son, but he would destroy the future God had promised him. The suffering of the old patriarch started when he said "Yes."

Look at David in that moment when he learns that Absalom, his beloved son, has organized a coup against him. See the pathos in David's face when he is told that Absalom is leading an uprising. Long before David's death, long before Absalom was killed in that battle, David started dying. There was anguish and suffering in his soul because one he loved more than life itself had turned against him, even his own flesh.

Do we not say that we suffer the loss of a friend or a loved one? We know the suffering that comes from spiritual and emotional loneliness of brutal proportions. We suffer disappointment, despair, even disillusionment. More than a few of us know what the saints of old wrote about when they described "the dark night of the soul." Such are the moments in our life when we feel as if the heavens are hammered brass, when we feel even God has turned a deaf ear to us. I call this soul pain the sacrament of suffering.

The word "sacrament" comes to us directly from the Latin language. The word *sacramentum* means to ordain or to consecrate. A sacrament is an act, a deed, a ritual believed to be the means of divine grace. A sacrament is a sign or symbol of spiritual reality. Baptists and other evangelicals don't traffic in sacraments. We Baptists are so averse to sacraments that we can't even find the word in our dictionary. We fear sacraments because we have associated them with priests. We Baptists have said we are all priests. Whether we warm to the word or not, every one of us has a deep need for sacraments in our lives. We need touchable, tangible, even tasteable, hearable, physical realities that tell us God is with us.

How many times have you been going through a difficult moment in your life when family member, a brother or a sister, or a member of the church family came up, put his or her arm around your shoulder, and held you close? Holding you close, they whispered in your ear, "I'm praying for you; I care for you." Understand that the person who said that could stand at a distance, look at you, and say, "I'm praying for you. I love you. I'm thinking about you." They could do that, but there is something powerful about human touch. Touch is sacramental.

Could it be, as C. S. Lewis believed, that suffering is a sacrament? Suffering is a sign, a symbol, a means by which God touches our lives. Through our human suffering God loves us, God touches us, God indeed comes near us. I'm not suggesting this morning that suffering has its genesis in God. I do not believe God visits the slings and arrows of this life upon us. I do believe deeply, however, that through suffering, the one universal reality we all know at some level, God loves us. I believe that through suffering we can be deeply, powerfully loved by God.

In one of his first books, *The Problem of Pain* (written in 1940), C. S. Lewis dealt with the whole issue of suffering, evil, and pain not only in human life but in all of life. At age forty-two, Lewis wrote the following: "Try to exclude the possibility of suffering and you find that you have excluded life itself." What is he saying? He is saying that suffering is woven into the fabric of life. Suffering is like oxygen in the air we breathe, cellulose in the pews on which we sit, sound in the music we sing. Suffering is of the very "thing-ness" of life. Yet, at times our suffering seems almost unbearable.

In Lewis's children's story *The Lion, The Witch, and the Wardrobe*, the heroine Lucy goes through a magic wardrobe. When she does, she finds herself in the land of Narnia. When she comes into Narnia, Lucy discovers that a blanket of snow covers all the land. It is cold, foreboding, almost lifeless. Lucy soon learns that Narnia is the place "where it is always winter but never Christmas."

How many of us know all about Narnia? There are times when life itself seems a cold, empty, foreboding winter. Not only is it never Christmas, but we don't even hear a Christmas carol being sung or played anywhere in the land. What if suffering is hardwired to our lives, and through suffering, through the winters of our life, we come to understand in greater ways the love of God?

In the same year that Lewis wrote *The Problem of Pain*, his dear friend Owen Barfield buried his mother. Owen Barfield, with C. S. Lewis, Charles Williams, J. R. R. Tolkien of *The Lord of the Rings*, brother Warren Lewis, and others formed a writer's group in Oxford called the Inklings. These men were close friends. They talked about their many writing projects in an Oxford pub called the Eagle and Child. Intimate friendships developed through this group. When Barfield's mother died, Lewis took pen and paper and wrote his friend a letter of consolation. In that letter, Lewis quotes the fifteenth century mystic Julian of Norwich. Said Julian in the fifteenth century, "All shall be well, and all shall be well, and all manner of thing shall be well."

In mid-letter, Lewis seems to catch himself. He realizes that he has thrown out a one-liner. He has offered good counsel from Julian, but he seems to realize that, even as strong as that lovely line is, it is not enough. He continues writing his friend. "The real difficulty, isn't it, is to adapt one's steady beliefs about tribulation to this particular tribulation." Here is the real challenge for all of us; to take our "one-line" theology about suffering and see if, amid some "particular tribulation," what we believe can carry us through the awful moment in which we find ourselves. We must adapt our general beliefs about life's suffering, difficulty, and pain to the particular tribulations through which we live.

What is God saying to us from the text and from our friend C. S. Lewis about suffering? For one, we do not suffer alone. I know many people do. Many suffer a brutal loneliness of the soul. You may be there now. You may be enduring the most difficult suffering of soul, of heart, of life, feeling as if no one else understands where you are.

There is a natural tendency in all of our lives when suffering comes to retreat into ourselves, to go into the secure cave of our own soul and say, "Listen, I can handle it. It is okay. Leave me alone." We often suffer alone, but we need not suffer alone. Such soul suffering need not be because God knows our sorrow. God has experienced our pain. God is with us. Jesus is Emmanuel, God with us. Jesus said, "I will never leave you or forsake you." The tendency in life is to withdraw, to step away, to isolate, when what Jesus and C. S. Lewis teach us, what the saints through the ages have told us, is if we simply open our hearts to God we discover we are not alone. One has gone before us who knows who we are and where we are.

I don't know if you miss him or not, but I still miss Lewis Grizzard. I know he was earthy and at times profane, but he had a way of saying the most profound truth in language that Southerners understood. Lewis Grizzard grew up as a Methodist in Moreland, Georgia. When he was a little boy, he asked his preacher, "Can you dig your way to hell?" "I guess you can," said the preacher, "but I can tell you how to get there a lot quicker."

If you and I in our suffering decide we are going to dig ourselves into the loneliness and isolation of our own little caves, we probably can get to where we are going eventually. You can, however, get to consolation a whole lot quicker if you will let the resources and person of Jesus Christ love you through your suffering.

What is our Lord teaching us? He says we can, if we choose, discover meaning in suffering. If sacrament is a means of divine grace, could it be that suffering is an arrow pointing to God? Perhaps suffering is pointing us to God, asking, "What are you learning from your suffering?" Don't waste your suffering. How are you growing and becoming the fuller person God created you to be?

All of us have marveled at the exploits of Lance Armstrong. Lance Armstrong is to cycling what Tiger Woods is to golf. He has won the Tours de

France multiple times. You may have forgotten that at the age of twenty-five, Armstrong was diagnosed with a virulent form of cancer. He underwent months of chemotherapy. According to Armstrong, after his chemotherapy he ate Mexican food, played golf, and lay on the couch. One day his wife Kristin said, "Lance, you need to decide something: Are you going to be a golf-playing, beer-drinking, Mexican-food-eating slob for the rest of your life?"

"This conversation," said Armstrong, "changed everything. Within days I was back on my bicycle." Then he goes on to say the most remarkable thing. Lance Armstrong said, "Without cancer I never would have won a single Tour de France. Cancer taught me a plan for more purposeful living, and then in turn taught me how to train and to win more purposefully. Pain and loss are great enhancers."[1] Suffering can, if we let it, teach us something about God.

Perhaps the dearest and most precious thing suffering teaches us is that God has gone before us in suffering love in the person of Jesus of Nazareth. If we follow him, we too will know that suffering and discover by his grace that we can endure it by faith.

Finally, the text is telling us that suffering need not crush us. I've told our three young adult children that the things in life that do not crush you only make you stronger. We read a text today in which our Lord said there was coming a time in his life when forces not of God would crush him, reject him, inflict great pain upon him, and kill him. That suffering would be a crushing moment. The disciples would witness the death of their beloved teacher and know grief unlike any they had known before. But it is the witness of our faith that what the world believed crushed Jesus Christ only made him stronger. By his stripes we are healed; through his death we come to know life.

No, this sacrament of suffering is not bucking up to a problem in your life. It is not a pep talk that will help you feel better. It is not wishful thinking that maybe the pain will go away. Rather, it is living in God through our lives. It is realizing that the pain through which we live can be a sacrament, a means by which God touches us.

In June 2002, our family learned that my dad had a debilitating illness. His bone marrow was not producing mature blood cells. A chart of his blood numbers looked like a ski slope that kept going down, down, down. His white count, red count, and platelets slid lower toward the right side of the chart. My dad had always been a vigorous, active man. But in his early eighties, he went from being vigorous, healthy, and energized, working and enjoying life, to a person without energy. It wasn't long after his diagnosis that I asked him, "Dad, how do you feel about all of this?" He said to me, "Tim, I've had a good ride. I know that God is with me and that God will be with me through whatever I have to face." I said,

"Tell me more, Dad." He said, "The real difficulty is not facing my death. I am ready to meet the Lord. The tough part is leaving your mother. She needs me now." My mom and dad have known each other since the sixth grade and have been married more than sixty years. "The tough part is leaving her and wanting to see all my grandchildren graduate from high school." Fifteen months after we had the conversation, my dad died into eternal life.

Did you hear what he said to me? It was not the dying where he met the reality of suffering. It was all the things through which he knew he would live before he awakened in that place that is only light and love. Mark it down. All of us will go through the experience of suffering. Sometimes it comes as physical affliction. Sometimes it comes as a dark night of the soul. Sometimes it comes in the ambiguities of human life. I do not know how it will come to you, but when it does, you will make a choice. You will decide in that moment whether or not you will fix your eyes fully and faithfully on the One who goes before you, whether you will follow this Jesus who says, "Take up your cross and follow me." If you will do that, my friend, "All will be well. And all will be well. And all manner of things will be well."

[1] Lance Armstrong, "Back in the Saddle," *Forbes* (12 December 2001).

From the Depths of Sin and Shame

They stripped him and put a scarlet robe on him, and after twisting some thorns into a crown, they put it on his head.
—Matthew 27:28-29

Palm Sunday is a thunderous shout that all too quickly becomes a murderous shriek. Seeing Jesus ride into the Holy City on Palm Sunday to a crowd's standing ovation demands that we ask, "Is this how God saves us?" Is this how God does God's work? A hero's parade, streets lined with happy children waving palm branches like pom-poms, cheers rising into a blue sky, hope smeared on expectant faces, deafening noise. Is this how God saves us?

Everything is in order, even planned. Willing people lending whatever the hero wants: a donkey, armfuls of cloaks for carpet, an upper room with an incredible view of the city for entertaining. Everything is neatly in place. Is this how God saves us? The disciples surely hoped it was. Three years of hearing about the kingdom of God, blind eyes seeing, lame legs walking, even dead bodies breathing. Three years of remembering the taste of bread and fish—that hillside, that day, those thousands fed.

Three years of breathing the air of anticipation thick with political promise, ripe for revolutionary reform. Three years of feeling the press of crowds, the electric atmosphere that followed Jesus wherever he went. Three years punctuated with hope and now this triumphal entry to the city of cities, the Holy City, Jerusalem. Could God's kingdom and God's promises be any nearer? They were right at their fingertips. God was there, wasn't he? God was there ready to run over the oppressors, right all the wrongs, turn over every perverse deal. This was it, wasn't it?

Through the years I've asked myself many times, "How does God save us?" I've heard many ideas. I've read the theologians. I've traveled down some paths that at first looked promising only to find them to be dead-end streets. I could give you a laundry list of eminent theologians and thinkers through the history of the Christian church who could tell you how and where and why God does God's saving work. But only recently did it hit me. Maybe where I am, maybe what I think, maybe what we believe has nothing to do with where God is or what God thinks or what God does. Maybe Holy Week is not about what we do as much it is about what he did and who he was.

Oh, yes, we did it. We shouted on Sunday for glory. We shouted on Friday for death. Yes, the human family nailed him to that cross. Never think in sterile terms that the Romans crucified Jesus or that ridiculous, insane notion that peppered through the Christian church for 2,000 years that the Jews killed Christ. It is so easy for us to believe such stupid ideas and never see that we are the ones who did the dirty deed. Our sin crucified Jesus. The collective human family's disobedience nailed Jesus to a cross.

Do you see it? The temptation is to focus on ourselves. It is the human thing to ponder what we believe and in what categories to believe it and all the while miss who he is, what he did, and why Jesus gave his life for us.

But he is the sinless Son of God. What happened to him would have been only an atrocity, a murder, a martyrdom had it not been that he is the Son of God. What happened to Jesus was horrible beyond description. It was evil at its highest level.

Because it was Jesus, his death is God's love written on Calvary's tree. The Bible says Jesus was the sinless One. He died so that all of us could live. John had it right at the beginning of his ministry when standing knee-deep in water, he saw Jesus coming to him, and said, "Behold the Lamb of God who takes away the sin of the world."

Jesus is the sinless Son of God. Never once did he raise his fist to strike someone in anger. Never once did he harbor animosity in his heart that would harm or maim, cripple or wound another person. Never once did he let that awful thing in our lives that wants to grab and to use, to control and even to destroy control him. Never once did Jesus sin and disobey God. He is the spotless Lamb of God, the sinless Christ. That's who he is and so much more.

But what did he do? He descended into the depths of sin and shame. The prophet Isaiah, with uncommon prescience, spoke words that now haunt our history: "Surely he has borne our griefs and carried our sorrows." The picture of

God that limps out of the Bible is a picture of God who is bruised and wounded, broken and beaten. God who is bleeding. God who is abandoned, shamed because of my sin and yours. God in Christ went to the depths of sin and shame for you and me.

Did you hear how Matthew described that awful scene in the Praetorium? He tells us they stripped him and, as he stood naked before those soldiers, placed the scarlet robe, a sign of monarchy, on his shoulders. They wove a crown of thorns and stuck it on his head. They put a staff in his right hand, the hand of authority. They spit on him. They mocked him. Then, with depraved cruelty, they took the staff out of his hand and struck him on the head again and again and again.

Do you still have the video playing in your mind of that awful crime in Los Angeles when policemen, out of control and fear, beat Rodney King? How they beat and kicked him, striking him repeatedly? That crime is mild compared to what the soldiers did to Jesus. They humiliated him. They made sport of him. They spit on him and then said, "Hail, king of the Jews."

How does God save us? God saves us in a lonely garrison on a Friday morning before people just like us who think they finally have God in their hands. There, from the depths of sin and shame, bleeding flesh on a stone floor, is where God saves us. Truth to tell, we would like to be saved by a hero on a white horse. How we would like to live into our fondest fantasies of being rescued by one who charges in with his armies. But that is not where God does God's work. God descended down, down, down, down into the depths of sin and shame for us.

One last, demanding question lingers. Why does God in Christ save us that way? The Bible says there is only one reason, a ludicrous reason at best. The Bible says that Jesus, the sinless Son of God, went to the depths of sin and shame because of love. The Christian gospel is all about love: radical love, outrageous love, earthy love, bleeding love. If you are uncomfortable with that or simply don't like it, Christianity is not your religion of choice. I could recommend a number of others.

The Christian faith is about being the loving presence of God when people are cruel. The Christian gospel is about being the loving, embracing presence of God when others are malicious. The Christian gospel is about bringing the human family together under the banner of crucified love even when we would seek to keep the family separate and at odds with each other. Read the Bible. Read it carefully. The Christian gospel is about reconciling the broken pieces lying on the floor of our troubled world and bringing them back together again under the Lordship of Jesus Christ. Why? Love.

Charles Gabriel said it so well. I guess I've read and sung this hymn dozens of times. "In loving kindness Jesus came my soul in mercy to reclaim; and from the depths of sin and shame thro' grace he lifted me." I've sung that first stanza from the time I was a child. It is like "Amazing Grace," "How Great Thou Art," "The Old Rugged Cross." You can sing it anywhere. You know the words. But it wasn't until recently that I realized what Charles Gabriel was saying. Ponder the words of that first stanza a bit more. Did you hear it?

"In loving kindness Jesus came my soul in mercy to reclaim." And then this line that haunts me still: "And from the depths of sin and shame." I always thought that was my sin and shame. I thought Gabriel was talking about me. We humans are incurably self-centered. But that is not what I believe he meant at all. Hear it again. "In loving kindness Jesus came my soul in mercy to reclaim. And from the depths of sin and shame." Whose sin? Whose shame?

Paul helps us. Said he, "For our sake [God] made [Jesus] to be sin who knew no sin, so that in him we might become the righteousness of God" (2 Cor 5:21). Looking beyond the veil of his own time, Isaiah wrote, "He was despised and rejected by others; a man of suffering and acquainted with infirmity" (Isa 53:3). Looking down the long, mysterious corridors of the future, the prophet talked about the shame of the crucified One. From the depths of sin and shame, Jesus lifted you and me.

The second stanza takes this thought one further step. "His head was bruised with many a thorn. His hands by cruel nails were torn; when from my grief and guilt forlorn, in love he lifted me. From sinking sand he lifted me, with tender hand he lifted me, from shades of night to plains of light, O praise his name, he lifted me!"

Palm Sunday smacks every idea in the head that suggests that you have to get cleaned up to come to God. Palm Sunday kicks this idea around the junkyard of human thought, smashes it, and buries it. Somehow we have mistakenly come to think and act as if God is the God only of respectable, clean, happy people. We think God comes along to dress up what is ugly and make it pretty. Palm Sunday tells us that we shout on Sunday and murder on Friday. But the Christ who goes into Jerusalem on Sunday knows there is an appointment with death on Friday. He goes from the height of Sunday to the depth of Friday to meet us where we are. So graphically depicted now in Mel Gibson's film *The Passion of the Christ*, our Lord descends into the depths of sin and shame for us. From those depths, the depths to which this Christ went, God saves us.

What about you? Are you still trying to convince everybody that you have it all together, that you can make it in your own strength? That grace and saving faith is really about what you think and what you believe and where you are going? Or would you journey again with Jesus through these last few days and put the light on Jesus and remember that it was for you, my friend, for all of us, he went to the depths of sin and shame. And because he went there, he can lift us, forgive us, and give us a new life. That's the story of Holy Week. It's the story that can become your story, your introduction to life, so much so that you can sing, "In loving-kindness Jesus came my soul in mercy to reclaim; and from the depths of sin and shame, thro' grace he lifted me."

Finding the Risen Lord

And very early on the first day of the week,
when the sun had risen, they went to the tomb.
—Mark 16:2

Each year during Holy Week I take a few minutes and reread the Easter stories as found in the four Gospels and 1 Corinthians 15. All four Gospels conclude with our Lord's resurrection. In fact, the Easter account is the compelling reason the four Gospels were written. If Christ is not risen in glory, there is no reason even to tell the story. Jesus would have been no more important, perhaps even less important, in history than Socrates or Plato, Marcus Aurelius or Betsy Ross. But because he lives, the four Gospels came to life and have life. Paul, in writing to the Corinthians, tells the story of glory, that Christ is alive and that even he was a witness to the risen Christ.

One of the things you discover when you read the accounts in the four Gospels—Matthew, Mark, Luke, and John—is that everybody seems to be in such a rush. No, the word "dash" comes to mind. The women start their journey early. They get up before the sun rises. John adds the poignant phrase "while it was still dark." In the wee hours before daylight, they make their way to the tomb. The stories muscle you into feeling the hurry in these women's steps. There is an urgency to their business. And a grim business it is. It is not a pretty thing they are going to do. They are going to do love's last act for their beloved teacher. They will anoint his body with spices in the custom of their people. It was women's work in that culture to tend to the dead, and they were going to do it faithfully.

When reading the Gospels of Luke and John, you discover that Peter puts on his Nikes and runs here and there, to and from the empty tomb. He is in a hurry.

All four Gospels tell us that everyone who leaves the tomb—the women, Peter, the beloved disciple—all who leave the tomb run, flee, dash from the cemetery. My question is, Why the hurry? Why are they running to and from the tomb? What is the rush?

At first the women hurried to complete their burial work. They came to the tomb expecting to find a corpse and they found the stone rolled away. But once they stooped down and looked in, once they heard the news, "He is not here. He is risen!" then the dash began. Everyone from that moment on hurried to find the risen Christ. They were on the ultimate Easter search. They were looking for Jesus Christ. But alas, he could not be found. Check it out for yourself. Not one person, not one disciple ended up finding the risen Christ.

Understand that there is much finding going on in the story. The search is on. The women find the tomb. According to the Fourth Gospel, Peter and John find the linen burial cloth. Mary finds an angel, in whose presence she weeps. But no one, not Mary or Mary Magdalene or Salome or Peter or John, no one finds the risen Christ. He is not found in the story. This Jesus-not-found suggests that we might not find him either.

Here is a sobering word for Easter.

One year during Holy Week, I had grocery duty. I do the grocery shopping every once in a while. Kathie bravely sends me off to do the shopping. So this week, it was my turn to go. I had a list of everything we needed. I don't know where things are in the grocery store nearly as well as she does. I have to ask people. I stop strangers. "Can you tell me where I might find the garbage bags?" You can almost hear women I ask saying to themselves, *Oh no, another man looking without success.*

Perhaps you saw the joke about the weapons inspectors in Iraq. "Why couldn't they find any weapons of mass destruction? Because the inspectors were all men." Men can't find anything. So there I am, list in hand, going up and down the aisles looking for things. I had this one item I needed to get but couldn't find. On the list was Honey Nut Cheerios. Everybody stocks Honey Nut Cheerios. I get to the cereal section and there are fifty kinds of cereal. I find the Cheerios section. I stand in front of it. There are regular Cheerios, Low-fat Cheerios, Multi-berry Cheerios, even Honey Nut Chek Cheerios. I find all manner of Cheerios, but I can't find the plain, simple, uncomplicated Honey Nut Cheerios. I read every cereal row from left to right in English. I then read each row from right to left in Hebrew. I read the rows in Chinese from top to bottom. I read the cereal list backwards and forwards.

I say to myself, *Here in Holy Week, you would think a respectable grocery store would have Honey Nut Cheerios.* They've got matzah, matzah ball soup mix by the case, lamb and ham, but no Honey Nut Cheerios. Frustrated, I take the full cart of groceries and head to the checkout counter and start putting my things on the conveyor belt. This helpful lady at the checkout counter says, "Was everything okay?" I say, "Well, I couldn't find the Honey Nut Cheerios." She said, "You are kidding." I answer, "No. I stood in front of the cereal section and read the rows in English, Hebrew, and Chinese, and couldn't find it." She continues checking my purchases.

After she puts the last item through the scanner, I look up and she is gone—not even a "good-bye, see you later." She just turns around and walks off. As I keep scanning the store for any sign of her, I see her head bobbing as she walks toward the cereal section. I say to myself, *She is going to check this out for herself. She is not going to work for a place that doesn't stock Honey Nut Cheerios.* She walks over there and about a minute later comes back with the regular and the jumbo-size Honey Nut Cheerios. I look at her and say, "You know, these stock boys are so fast these days." Not amused, she says, "I've got people waiting, sir, which one do you want?"

This looking-but-not-finding part of the story is key to the Easter reality. Here is the story of all stories about people looking for the risen Christ. But I say it again: Not a one of them finds him. They look, but their looking never leads to finding. In fact, they do not find him until he first finds them.

Here is the Easter message we most need in our lives. We need it more than we can ever possibly imagine. It is this picture of God who finds us in our looking. Look at the facts of the story. Here is God finding the lifeless, cold Jesus and transforming death into life eternal. Contrary to what we might imagine, even in our most imaginative moments, the resurrection of Jesus is not the work of Jesus. All of the verbs in the story are in the passive voice. The resurrection act is something done to our Lord. Jesus has been raised. God has raised Jesus from the dead. This is the work of God who brings life out of death.

Simply put, we cannot and never will find the risen Lord. Our best hope, in fact, our only hope is that he finds us in our looking. And yes, if the stories tell us anything, they tell us that he can only find us if we are looking. No story in the New Testament suggests the risen Lord found anyone who wasn't, in some sense, first looking for him.

It is a fascinating turn of events, this finding and being found. Mary goes to the tomb looking for a body and is found by the Lord. Peter goes to the tomb and is found by the Lord. Paul, looking for trouble on the Damascus Road, is found by the living Lord. So how does he find us? That is what I want you to wrestle with at Easter. If you find yourself in a church on Easter, you are looking for something, too.

Don't we come to church on Easter looking, listening, wanting, needing? Of course we do. How does Jesus find us? The story bubbles up answers. The stories tell us he first finds us in our confusion. I thought about how confused we can be in our Christian faith. We will never remove ourselves from being encapsulated in the human package. You say, "I'm a Christian, but I still struggle with sins X, Y, and Z." My friend, welcome to the human family. You will struggle with some things all of your life. Some you will find victory over; others you will simply limp along with forever. If you are ever doubtful about whether you are truly human, just take a sharp pin and prick yourself. You will bleed like everybody else.

There is something about human nature, the human being, about you and me that confuses things. For example, we look for Jesus in the wrong place with the right motive. People traffic through my life, as they do yours, every day. They come through my life as a minister often carrying heavy burdens. Life has been cruel and difficult for them. From time to time some of the difficulties that people face have been self-wrought. Trouble comes to their lives by their own misbehavior or poor decisions. We all make them, don't we? Something I have discovered is that all of us tend to look in the wrong place for the right reason.

This is why people find themselves in all kinds of dysfunctional behaviors from alcoholism to gambling to affairs to all kinds of addictive, hurtful behaviors. They are looking for deep meaning in life. Mind you, they have the right reason, but they are looking in the wrong places. We all are guilty of acting this way. The deep need in our life is for relationship with God, for connection with others, for a personal understanding of the One who made us and in whose image we are made. And yet we go looking for him in the wrong places.

Do you know what else we do? We also look for him in the right place for the wrong reason. You may come to church—the right place—but you come to church for the wrong reason. You say, "How do people do that?" We do it all the time. I know folks who pick up the Bible—a very good thing to do—but they pick up the Bible for the wrong reason. I have had people stop me, total strangers, and say, "You're a preacher, aren't you?" I say, a bit sheepishly, "I am." Even when I have a golf shirt on, I am found out. "I've got a question for you."

What follows is almost predictable. They have taken the Bible, opened it up as if it were some kind of magic book with incantations or one-liners that will make what is wrong right. They ask, "Preacher, what do you think about 'so-and-so'?" Or, "Doesn't the Bible say this or that?" They are confused. They are looking for Jesus in the right place but for the wrong reason.

The women did that. They were at the right place. They came to the tomb. But he wasn't there. They were going to finish the burial ritual. They had no idea he would be alive. Jesus Christ comes and finds us in our confusion. Easter is the day we celebrate the wonderful good news that a simple, powerful message cleans up all the confusion, lifts all the fog, brings all the sunshine out. It is really simple. He is risen! It doesn't get any simpler than that.

Where does he find us? He finds us in our guilt. Guilt is a terrible thing. It is a crippler, a disabler. But guilt is part of the human package. You don't live long without having a little guilt in your life. Guilt is a tenured resident. It moves in with a never-ending lease. It is always there.

This was Peter's problem. Peter went looking for Jesus. He went trying to find Jesus, but Peter was looking for Jesus because he felt so guilty. Do you remember why? As he warmed his hands by that charcoal fire and people asked him about whether he knew the Lord, he said, "I don't know him. I don't know him. I don't know him," and the rooster crowed. Then guilt started pecking at his heart just like a rooster would.

The risen Christ finds us in our guilt. He comes to us with our hearts laden by the things we have done that we should not have done, the things we said that we should not have said, the places we went where we had no business going. Whereas you and I would pile the guilt on other people to control them, Jesus lifts the guilt from them and all of us. Where does he find us? He finds us in our guilt to set us free.

Where does he find us? He finds us in our grief. See Mary weeping in the garden. You remember the story as told by the Gospel of John. She finds the empty tomb. She doesn't know where Jesus' body is. She is confused. She may be a bit guilt-stricken. Perhaps she was saying to herself, "Maybe if I had gotten here sooner I could have protected him." She is standing in the garden weeping when a person she thinks is the gardener comes up behind her. He speaks. "Mary." She thought it was the gardener, but when he says, "Mary," she turns around and says, "My Teacher." Where does the risen Christ find us? He finds us in our grief.

We not only grieve the death of those we love, we start grieving the death of those we love before they die. We grieve the loss of job and the loss of innocence. We grieve the maturation process of our children. We are grateful they grow up, but we do grieve when they leave. Our Lord finds us in our grief, and when he does he calls our name. He comes to us. And when he does, the sun rises and never sets because Christ is alive.

Finally, in an ultimate sense, he finds us in our dying. All of us are dying. We are dying today. A hundred years from now, none of us will be here unless we are incredibly fortunate. We are all dying. Because we are dying, whether it is Easter or a hot summer day in July, a crisp, cool, October evening, or a wonderful

Christmas morning, whether it is that tender time at a deathbed or that tough moment at the graveside, Jesus Christ comes to us.

Augustine was right long ago when he said, "Our hearts are restless 'til they find their rest in Thee." We are restless human beings who search fanatically, adamantly, vigorously, passionately looking for God. We look in the wrong places for the right reasons. We look in the right places for the wrong reasons. We look with our guilt and we look in our guilt. We look in our grieving and in our dying. But it is not until we look up that we discover God is already looking for us.

For our part—this day and every day—we must decide whether or not we will be found. That is what you must decide. You must decide whether or not you will let this risen, living Christ find you. You can play your games with God. You can go here and go there and think this and think that, you can get on with your so-called life any way you want to, but the bottom line is, will you let God find you?

A long time ago, when I was a teenager, I sat down with my pastor like young people come and talk with me, and said, "I don't think I know the Lord." We got on our knees in his office and I prayed a simple prayer: "God, I'm a sinner and I'm lost and I need you." In that moment Jesus found me in a pastor's study just like he found Peter by the seaside and found Mary in the garden and found everyone who ever wanted to follow him exactly where they were. He found me and began changing my life.

"I was lost, but Jesus found me, found the sheep that went astray; threw his loving arms around me, drew me back into his way." Because he lives, my friend, you too can live. In fact, today, if you will let him, he will find you. He will put those risen arms around you and tell you, "You can live free now and forever." Let it be so for you. Let the Easter good news be the news that changes your life beginning today.

Printed in the United States
58708LVS00005B/304-324

9 781573 12444